From the Middlegame into the Endgame

From the Middlegame into the Endgame

by

Edmar Mednis
International Grandmaster

First published in 1994 by Gloucester Publishers plc, (formerly Everyman Publishers plc), Northburgh House, 10 Northburgh Street, London, EC1V 0AT

Copyright © 1994 E. Mednis

Reprinted 1996, 2003, 2005

British Library Cataloguing-in-Publication Data
A catalogue record for this book is available from the British Library.

ISBN 1 85744 060 9

Distributed in North America by The Globe Pequot Press, P.O Box 480, 246 Goose Lane, Guilford, CT 06437-0480.

All other sales enquiries should be directed to Everyman Chess, Northburgh House, 10 Northburgh Street, London, EC1V 0AT

tel: 020 7253 7887 fax: 020 7490 3708
email: info@everymanchess.com
website: www.everymanchess.com

EVERYMAN CHESS SERIES (formerly Cadogan Chess)

Chief Advisor: Garry Kasparov
Commissioning Editor: Byron Jacobs

Printed by Lightning Source

To
Sari and Mariss

Preface

Most chess books are written on a single subject. It is simply easier that way. Yet in the real life of actually playing a game you have to be concerned with the various aspects of the opening middlegame and endgame. In my first book for Pergamon Press, *From the Opening into the Endgame*, I showed how it is possible to go directly from the opening into the endgame, essentially bypassing the middlegame.

Of course, most games do contain a middlegame. The single most importantegic question that arises in middlegame play is: should I stay in the middlegame or aim for the endgame? Moreover, there are secondary questions associated with this primary one, such as: how is the answer affected by the quality of may position, i.e. superior, inferior, equal? One of the two objectives of this book is to tell you when to aim for the endgame and when to remain in the middlegame—no matter whether your position is superior, equal or inferior.

If the correct decision is to simplify into the endgame, what you need then are the tools for playing such endgames. This means knowing how to wierior endgames and how to hold inferior endgames. This then is the second objective of the book.

Therefore, the two objectives ot the book are: (1) to help you decide whether you should enter the endgame, and (2) if the anser is yes, how to win a superior endgame and draw an inferior one. Because the skills of playing endgames are independent ones. I have started the book with these parts, I mean, it does not really matter how or why you get into an endgame—you still have to play it correctly!

Some of the material in this book is based on work previously published by me in chess magazines, dealing with aspects of endgame play. Howere, in every case the material has been reviewed, expanded and updated to that it is of maximum immediate usefulness to the purchaser of this book. In general, the following standard sources have been utilized in the preparation of this book: personal knowledge, personal contacts and leading chess books and periodicals. When appropriate, direct credit is given given in the text.

To ensure that the reader and the author are on the same wavelength regarding the meaning of the question and exclamation marks as they are used in the characterization of moves, these are the presently accepted meanings:

! = a strong move

!! = a very strong move; a fantastic move

? = a bad move; a weak move

?? = a horrible move; a blunder

!? = an enterprising move; a move worthy of consideration

?! = a dubious move, for theoretical or practical reasons

As always, my deepest gratitude goes to my wonderful blonde wife, Baiba, not only for typing the entire manuscript but for never-ending physical and moral support.

In an undertaking of such scope, some errors are almost inevitable. The author accepts responsibility for all of these. Your assistance in bringing them to my attention will be appreciated.

New York, 1986

EDMAR MEDNIS

Contents

Part I

Introduction into Endgame Play

Even to the relatively uninitiated, the terms opening and middlegame are clear and are correctly understood. It is only "endgames" which have a mysterious aura about them. Since the major theme of the book involves entering endgames from middlegame positions, it is absolutely essential that the student understand what the endgame is about. The necessary background information is presented in the chapters that follow.

1

What is an Endgame?

Why is endgame study important?

One important—though fairly obvious—reason for studying endgames is that there is nothing thereafter. You can hope to rectify an opening error by excellent middlegame play. A middlegame error can perhaps be rectified by knowledgeable endgame play. But an error in the endgame is the ultimate error, turning a won position into a draw (and sometimes even into a loss!) or a tenable position into a loss. The other major reason is that endgame play is so inherently different from opening and middlegame play. Openings lead into middlegames so smoothly that very often the border is more or less arbitrary. Moreover, the difference is essentially academic, since the same general principles apply to both of these phases: the importance of the center, rapid and efficient piece development, king safety. Yet in the endgame these factors are only noteworthy by their absence.

What is an endgame?

Therefore, we want to know when we have reached the endgame, but how to determine this? The first point to make is that mechanical methods are suspect and will often lead to false conclusions. For instance, some of the early computer programs had both kings rushing for the center as soon as move 40 was reached because it was assumed that the endgame *must* have started by then! Such "play" is comical in its appearance and tragic in its result. A well-known computer manufacturer was using the following formula for a long time: the endgame program is activated when one side had 14 "points" remaining on the board and its king ventured out when the enemy had only 11 "points" remaining. (*Note*: in this point count only pieces—not

3

pawns—were considered.) The exchange (or lack of exchange) of the queen also provides no clear answer, since we definitely can have queenless middlegames and by definition there exist queen + pawn (and queen + minor piece) endgames.

Humans, because of their ability to think, should use a "thinking person's" approach to determine whether an endgame exists. You are likely to be in an endgame if the following conditions exist:

(1) Some exchange of material has taken place.
(2) Both kings look safe.
(3) Developmental and central factors are not of particular significance.

I believe that the single over-riding item is that of king safety. Not only is the king inherently safe in an endgame position, but even more to the point, the king should be centralized and utilized as a potentially valuable attacker.

The above guidelines will now be applied to the following three positions:

1. *Queen's Gambit Declined, Tartakover Variation*

1	d4	d5
2	c4	e6
3	Nc3	Nf6
4	Bg5	Be7
5	Nf3	0–0
6	e3	h6
7	Bh4	b6
8	cxd5	Nxd5
9	Bxe7	Qxe7
10	Nxd5	exd5
11	Rc1	Qb4+?
12	Qd2	Qxd2+
13	Kxd2!	

The correct evaluation of this position shows the following:

(a) Queens and two sets of minor pieces have been exchanged.
(b) White's king is quite safe on d2 and Black's castled king is obviously safe also.

These facts lead to the conclusion that we are in an endgame. Moreover, this endgame is significantly favorable for White because:

(1) Black's c-pawn is very weak—primary reason.
(2) White has the more active (centralized) king—secondary reason.

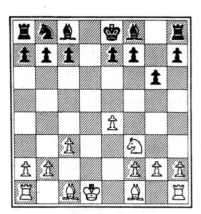

With this perspective in mind, we can see that:

(1) Black was quite wrong to play 11 . . . Qb4+? and exchange queens, since this makes it so much easier for White to attack Black's c-pawn.
(2) White was quite right in recapturing with his king (13 Kxd2!) since this centralizes the king, allows the rooks to be united and keeps the knight actively placed on f3 from where it can go to e5 to menace Black's c-pawn after the inevitable 13 . . . c6.

2. *English Opening, Andersson–Böök Variation*

1 c4	Nf6
2 Nc3	d5
3 cxd5	Nxd5
4 Nf3	g6
5 e4	Nxc3
6 dxc3	Qxd1+
7 Kxd1	

Even though only 6½ moves have occurred, already much has trans-

pired, so that the following firm conclusions can be made:

(a) The queens and one pair of knights have left the board.
(b) The rather solid pawn structure and Black's lack of development mean that White's king is safe on d1; similar reasoning also shows Black's king to be safe.
(c) Therefore, we can already consider this to be an endgame. White has the kind of normal slight advantage that is typical of modern opening play for the following reasons:

White's king will find an excellent centralized location on c2.
Both of White's bishops will find good diagonals. On the other hand, if Black fianchettoes his king's bishop, it will be biting on granite.

The e4 pawn gives White some central space, whereas Black's g6 pawn can turn out to be a slight weakening of the kingside.

3. *King's Indian Defense, Normal Variation*

1	d4	Nf6
2	c4	g6
3	Nc3	Bg7
4	e4	d6
5	Nf3	0–0
6	Be2	e5
7	dxe5	dxe5
8	Qxd8	Rxd8
9	Bg5	Na6
10	Nd5	Rd6
11	Bxf6	Bxf6
12	b4?!	c6
13	Nxf6+	Rxf6
14	a3	Bg4

A correct reading of this scene shows the following:

(a) The queens and two sets of minor pieces have been exchanged.

(b) Black's development is complete and his castled king is safe.

(c) White's 12 b4?! was unproductive and led to a further loss of time with 14 a3.

(d) White is clearly behind in development, his king is in the center and his rooks are unconnected. Yet since the position is rather closed and safe, these developmental factors are not of any real significance. With a normal sound sequence such as 15 Rd1 Re8 16 Nd2 White keeps equality in a rather harmless endgame.

However, in the game M. Knezevic – I. Zaitsev, Dubna 1976, White completely misjudged the position and played *15 Nxe5?* He thinks that the reduction of material means that he is already in a safe endgame, *even if he opens up the position.* But this is clearly suicidal, since now the backward development takes on mammoth importance. Black quickly gained a significant edge as follows: *15 . . . Bxe2 16 Kxe2 Re8 17 Nf3 Rxe4+ 18 Kd3 Rg4! 19 Rhg1 c5! 20 h3 Rgf4.* Black's rooks exert strong pressure against White's position and White's king in the middle of the board is much more of a liability than a strength. Black went on to win in 40 moves.

What is an endgame about?

During opening and middlegame play the primary emphasis is on effectively developing and using one's pieces and the primary object of attack is the enemy king. As a simplification we can say that the "pieces are king" and that the king is nothing but a continuous problem.

In the endgame everything is turned around. As already mentioned earlier, the king becomes an important attacking piece. Mikhail Tal, for example, has suggested that the value of an active king in the endgame is 3 points, i.e. equivalent to a knight or bishop.

The other major aspect of endgames is pawn play. As the number of pieces decreases, the importance of pawns increase. Each pawn placement can turn out to be of critical importance, since there is no way of correcting a misplacement by moving the pawn back! *The ultimate objective of endgame play is to queen a pawn.* Therefore, the side with the advantage—be it material or positional—has as its first broad objective the creation of a passed pawn, and as its ultimate objective the shepherding of the pawn into the 8th rank. Conversely, the defender must try to prevent this and his final defensive method often consists of giving up a knight or a bishop for the passed pawn to reach the drawn king + minor piece vs king position.

2

Mating Attacks in Endgames

In the previous chapter I made the point that in endgames the king becomes a potent attacking force and that he should be activated and used fully. Moreover, I suggested there that the single largest difference between middlegames and endgames is the lack of danger to the king in the endgame from a sudden mating attack. As a general strategic principle it is quite true that rather than be sheltered, the king should be activated in the endgame. But, because chess is such a rich and inherently inexhaustible game, one must nevertheless always be on the lookout for some tactical possibility which can negate the general principle of king safety in the endgame. These possibilities will occur less than 5% of the time, but they will occur, and it is very painful to be hit by an unexpected tactical shot.

The best example of this from master play is what happens from Diagram 4, Andersson – Hartston, Hastings 1972/3, after White's 35th move. The Swedish grandmaster

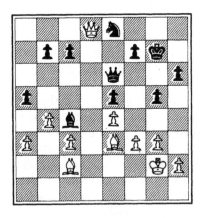

4

had just actively played his queen to d8; nevertheless, the position remains in balance, because neither side has any fundamental weakness and both sides have equivalently good piece placements. With his next move Black activates his knight:

35 . . .   Nf6!

Black's "normal" looking move contains an actual threat. This is, of course, easy to parry by, for example, 36 Qd1 or 36 Qd2. However . . .

36 Qxc7??

In such a "simple" position there can't be anything for Black—so White thinks. Yet shouldn't he have been suspicious of Black's *voluntary* placing the c-pawn *en prise*?

36 . . .   Qh3+!!
White resigns

The only choice is between accepting a "poetic" mate after 37 Kxh3 Bf1 or a prosaic one after 37 Kh1 Qf1+ 38 Bg1 Qxf3.

What could be considered another example of "self-mate" occurs from Diagram 5, Turoverov – Arzumanyan, USSR 1975 Corres-

5

pondence, after Black's 40th move. Black has the active position on the kingside, White has pressure on the queenside and over-all the chances are about equal. However, White,

spying that Black's knight on a6 is unprotected, sees the chance for a breakthrough:

41 c5   Bxb5!

After Black's accurate reply, White has nothing better than to continue with the modest 42 Nxb5. Then 42 . . . dxc5?! is dangerous because of 43 d6! cxd6 44 Nxd6 and White will win either the b-pawn or the e-pawn. However, steady equality is provided by 42 . . . bxc5 and neither side has anything better than to repeat moves with 43 Na7 Nb8 44 Nb5 Na6 etc. White wants more, continues his "combination", yet gets quite a shock.

42 cxd6??

If Black would have to recapture this pawn, White would stand great after 43 Nxb5, but Black can play the "naive" . . .

42 . . .   Bxf1!

and after

43 d7

comes the unexpected

43 . . .   Nc5!

If White doesn't queen, he'll be a piece down. Yet after

44 d8(Q)

there is the shocking

44 . . .   Nd3+!!
45 Kxf1   Ng3
Mate

Of course, mates with minor pieces are generally rare and "accidental mates" such as the previous two cases even more so. Most of the mates occur as a logical consequence of the position at hand. For this type, a good example is Diagram 6, I. Zaitsev – Bakulin, USSR 1964, Black to move. The h-pawn

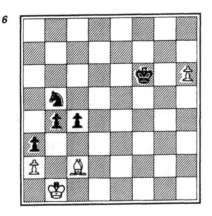

6

ties down Black's king, but on the queenside Black has a 3 P vs 1 P majority and White's king looks quite contained. Black won as follows:

1 . . .   Nc3+
2 Ka1   Kf7
3 h7   Kg7

White is now in zugzwang and can't prevent Black's decisive . . . b3. He does try one last small trick.

4 Bd3

So that after 4 . . . cxd3?? 5 h8(Q)+ Kxh8 White has been stalemated. However, after the thematic

4 . . .   b3
White resigns

After 5 axb3 cxb3 there is nothing to be done about 6 . . . b2 mate.

The presence on the board of a rook significantly increases the chance for a mating attack. The position in Diagram 7, Lucko – Belousenko, USSR 1976, after

7

White's 63rd move, is bare bones and yet presents Black with a creative opportunity. Of course, theoretically the position is drawn as there is no forcible method for Black to realize his extra pawn. Ever observant, Black tries the innocuous-looking:

63 . . .   Re3!?

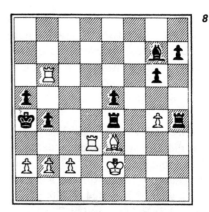

In fact, Black does *not* have a threat and White can choose the "active" 64 Ra2+ or keep the status quo with 64 Rb1—in either case the position remains drawn. Yet White, under the impression that "anything draws", carelessly plays . . .

64 Ra4??

. . . and is skewered by

64 . . .   Rh3+!!
White resigns

He is mated after 65 gxh3 g3+ 66 Kh1 g2+ 67 Kh2 g1(Q)+.
The above elementary combination is an important one and can be equally applicable to more complicated endgames. Consider first Diagram 8, Shablinsky – Ushkal, USSR 1974, White to move and mate. The solution:

1 Ra3+!!   bxa3
2 b3
Mate

A more sophisticated execution of this same motif is from Diagram 9, Moldojarov – Samochanov, 1974 USSR Correspondence, after

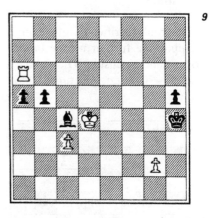

Black's 65th move. By itself, White's slight material advantage is insufficient to win, because Black has a passed a-pawn and White can't eliminate it by 66 Rxa5, since

Black then plays 66 . . . Kg3 and will obtain a passed h-pawn. There is for White, however, the opportunity to try to weave a mating net:

66 Rg6	a4

Black allows our "main line" mate. Yet there is no satisfactory defence. Even though 66 . . . Bf7 67 Rg7 Be6 is a better try, White still has a mating attack after 68 Ke3 Bg4 69 Kf4 a4: 70 Re7! a3 71 Rel followed by 72 Rhl+.

67 Ke3	a3
68 Kf4	a2
69 Rg3!	Be6
70 Rh3+!!	Bxh3
71 g3	
Mate	

This rook sacrifice motif is equally applicable further up the board. For instance, consider Diagram 10, Durao – Catozzi, Portugal 1957,

White to move. Black's king may appear reasonably safe, yet White mates in three:

1 Rf4+	Kh5
2 Rh4+!!	gxh4
3 g4	
Mate	

If the rook has the help of a minor piece, more opportunities for mating arise. A classical example from long ago is shown in Diagram 11, Rotlevi – Farni, Carlsbad 1911, after Black's 79th move. Black had

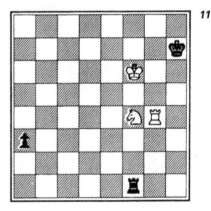

11

defended this R vs R+N endgame quite badly and now finds himself in a mating net:

80 Kf7	Kh6

Or 80 . . . Rh1 81 Nd5! a2 82 Nf6+ followed by 83 Rg6 mate.

10

81 Kg8!
Black resigns

There is nothing to be done about 82 Rg6 mate. Note that in this final position Black's a-pawn is a severe handicap to him. Without it, he could play the saving 81 . . . Rg1! and if White captures, it's stalemate!

A more modern example, where the defending side is handicapped by the presence of a pawn, is Diagram 12, Chistyakov – Kremenetsky, Moscow 1968, after White's

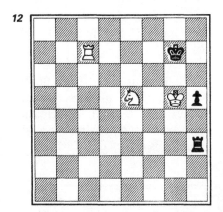

12

64th move. Obviously Black's king is in check and must move—but to which one of the three possible squares?

64 . . .   Kg8??

Not here! And also not 64 . . . Kh8?? because of the ob-

vious 65 Kh6 Rg3 66 Rc8+ Rg8 67 Ng6 mate. Sufficient to hold the draw was 64 . . . Kf8! and after 65 Kf6, 65 . . . Kg8. Then neither 66 Rg7+ Kf8 nor 66 Ng6 Rf3+ 67 Kg5 Rf7! lead to success for White.

65 Ng6!
Black resigns

But here—thanks to the h-pawn—White can't be prevented from playing the decisive 66 Kh6, followed by 67 Rg7 mate. For instance, 65 . . . Rf3 66 Kh6 Rf7 67 Rc8+ Rf8 68 Rxf8 mate.

A fine illustration of a surprising K + R + N mating attack by a world champion occurs from Diagram 13, Em. Lasker – Schiffers, Nurenberg 1896, after Black's 42nd

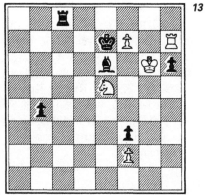

13

move. White does have a far advanced f-pawn, but there is no way to queen it. As a matter of fact,

Black could have blockaded it on his previous move by playing 42 . . . Rf8. But seeing no danger, he decided to follow the "passed pawns must be pushed" principle and he had carelessly advanced the b-pawn. The punishment by Lasker is swift:

**43 f8(Q)+!!   Kxf8
44 Kf6**

Suddenly Black's king is caught in a mating net and there is no defense. Consider the following variations:

(1) 44 . . . Re8 45 Rh8+ Bg8 46 Ng6 mate.
(2) 44 . . . Kg8 45 Rg7+ Kf8 (45 . . . Kh8?? 46 Ng6 mate) 46 Re7! Bd5 (or 46 . . . Bf5 47 Rf7+ and White wins the bishop and keeps the bind) 47 Ng6+ Kg8 48 Rg7 mate.
(3) 44 . . . Bd5 45 Rh8+ Bg8 46 Ng6+ Ke8 47 Rxg8+ Kd7 48 Ne5+ Kc7 49 Rxc8+ Kxc8 50 Nxf3 b3 51 Nd2 b2 52 Kg6 Kd7 53 f4 and the passed f-pawn wins.

Black tries a fourth defense, which is equally hopeless.

**44 . . .   Bg8
45 Re7!   Bh7**

There was nothing else to be done about the dual threats of 46 Nd7 mate and 46 Ng6 mate. 45 . . . Bd5 allows 46 Ng6+ Kg8 47 Rg7 mate.

**46 Rxh7   Kg8
47 Rg7+   Kf8
48 Rb7   Ra8
49 Rf7+!   Ke8
50 Re7+
Black resigns**

His choice is between being mated via 50 . . . Kf8 51 Ng6+ Kg8 52 Rg7 or by 50 . . . Kd8 51 Nf7+ Kc8 52 Nd6+ Kd8 (52 . . . Kb8 53 Rb7 mate) 53 Ke6 followed by 54 Rd7.

It is in endgames having double rooks that the question of king safety starts to assume increasing importance. What is almost a model situation is depicted in Diagram 14,

14

Machek – Kas, 1976 Yugoslavia – Hungary Women's match, White to move. White's material advantage is of small importance because Black is sure to gain at least one of the pawns back. Yet with Black's king contained on his first rank, White's king + rooks active, there is the chance for an immediate mating attack:

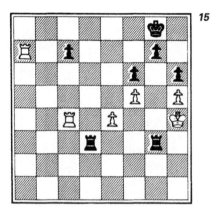

15

1 Rg2+	**Kf8**

If 1 . . . Kh8 2 Kf6! Rxf2 (or 2 . . . Rd6+ 3 Kf7 etc.) 3 Ra8+ Kh7 4 Rg7+ Kh6 5 Rh8 mate.

2 Ke6!	**Re2+**

Or 2 . . . Rxa2 3 Rf7+ Ke8 4 Rg8 mate; or 2 . . . Rd8 3 Rf7+ Ke8 4 Rg8 mate.

3 Kf6
Black resigns

There is no defense to the mating threat of 4 Rf7+ Ke8 5 Rg8.
Or the king can be caught on the edge of the board as in Diagram 15, Gerusel – Malich, Leipzig 1975, after White's 37th move:

37 . . .	**Rg5!**
38 Rcxc7	

The immediate mate could have been prevented by 38 Raxc7 Rdg3 39 e5 Rg1! 40 Rc3 though after

40 . . . fxe5 followed by winning the f-pawn Black would be two pawns up with an easy win.

38 . . .	**Rdg3!**
White resigns	

There is no rational defense to 39 . . . Rdg4 mate.
Even where the king looks secure, combinational motifs often are feasible to demonstrate otherwise. Material is even and Black's position looks reasonable in Diagram 16, Chiburdanidze – Feustel, Tiflis 1976, after Black's 41st move. However, White fashioned a mating net as follows:

42 f4	**Rc2**
43 Rg7+	**Kf6**
44 g5+!	**hxg5**
45 Rgf7+	**Kg6**
46 f5+	
Black resigns	

16

Black's new g-pawn takes away a fleeing square from his king, thus causing mate after 46 . . . Kh5 47 Rh7.

Being on the look-out for mating opportunities can sometimes make the technical job of winning considerably easier. A good example is Diagram 17, Mednis – Kaimo, New York (GHI) International 1977,

17

after Black's 52nd move. White now could play 53 Rxh7, which theoretically should be good enough for the win, though it is clear that after 53 . . . Kf4! Black's king has become active and he obtains some real practical chances. Therefore, White finds a way to leave Black "chanceless":

| 53 Kg3! | h6 |

The threat was 54 h4+ Kh6 55 Rxh7 mate.

54 h4+	Kh5
55 Kh3!	Be2
56 Rf4	e5

To prevent mate, Black must give up his bishop, as 56 . . . g5 is refuted by 57 g4+ Kg6 58 h5 mate.

57 g4+	Bxg4+
58 Rxg4	e4
59 Rf4	

Good enough, of course, but much more in the spirit of my theme would have been 59 Rg5+!! hxg5 60 Rh7 mate!

59 . . .	e3
60 Rb1	e2
61 Re1	
Black resigns	

3

What is an "Equal Endgame"?

The emphasis in this book is on superior and inferior endgames, since these are the endgames resulting when a player makes a *major* decision to terminate the middlegame and enter the endgame. But of course real life is full of equal endgames. Some of these occur "naturally" enough, whereas others come about because one side is truly playing for a draw or simply prefers the relative safety of an endgame.

In chess literature evaluations of endgame positions often end up with the equality sign. Does this mean that the game should therefore be abandoned as a draw? No, not necessarily. What does it mean? It can mean a number of things and it is always very important for the practical player to get the correct meaning.

The three types of equality are: (1) practical, (2) theoretical, (3) dynamic. There are positions where more than one "equality" is present, but then *one* of the "equali-

ties" is usually still *the* dominant one.

Practical equality means that the position is so simple and clear that it is impossible to lose. The player with an inferior position should always aim for such a situation. A perfect example of this procedure from the highest level of competition is shown from Diagram 18, R. Fischer – B. Spassky, 1972 World

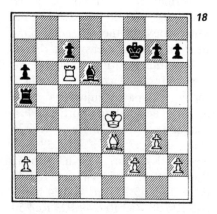

18

Championship Match, Game 16, after Black's 27th move. Though

material is even, White's position is
uncomfortable since Black has an
active rook and a passed c-pawn. If
White now plays the passive 28
Rc2, Black responds with
28 . . . Ke6, followed by Ra4+ and
Kd5 and has a very powerful active
position.

Therefore, Fischer prefers a
pawn down R + P endgame, which
is a certain practical draw:

28 Bf4!	Ra4+
29 Kf3	Ra3+
30 Ke4!	Rxa2
31 Bxd6	cxd6
32 Rxd6	Rxf2
33 Rxa6	Rxh2
34 Kf3!	

with *practical* equality.

Normal R + 2P vs R + 1P
endgames, with all the pawns on the
same side and the defending king
near its pawn, are easy sure draws.
In fact this position could be im-
mediately called a draw. It is only to
repay for past "injustices" that
Spassky decided to "torture" Fis-
cher (34 . . . Rd2 35 Ra7+ Kf6 36
Ra6+ Ke7 37 Ra7+ Rd7 38 Ra2
Ke6 39 Kg2 Re7 40 Kh3 Kf6 41
Ra6+ Re6 42 Ra5 h6 43 Ra2 Kf5 44
Rf2+ Kg5 45 Rf7 g6 46 Rf4 h5 47
Rf3 Rf6 48 Ra3 Re6 49 Rf3 Re4 50
Ra3 Kh6 51 Ra6 Re5 52 Kh4 Re4+
53 Kh3 Re7 54 Kh4 Re5 55 Rb6
Kg7 56 Rb4 Kh6 57 Rb6 Re1 58

Kh3 Rh1+ 59 Kg2 Ra1 60 Kh3 Ra4
Draw).

Theoretical equality means that *if*
the inferior side defends perfectly,
he will draw. For instance, the basic
endgame of R + B vs R is a
theoretical draw. However, the defender has to expect 100 (!) moves
of careful, unpleasant defending.
Often just a slight error is enough to
land one into a theoretically *lost*
position. Another common example is R + f- and h-pawns vs R
where the defending king is in a
good defensive position near the
pawns. All such positions are played out for a long time and the
defender has to play extremely well
to draw.

From a *practical* standpoint, such
theoretically drawn endgames
should only then be entered if there
is nothing better. In practice they
are much more difficult to draw
than endgame books claim.

Dynamic equality simply means
that the *chances* are equal. Either
side can readily win such positions if
it plays better than the opponent. It
is just as easy to win (or to lose!) a
dynamically equal endgame as a
dynamically equal middlegame
position.

A relatively simple position is
shown in Diagram 19, K. Regan –
L. Christiansen, 1978 US Championship, after Black's 26th move.

(see following diagram)

White has the queenside pawn majority, whereas Black has the somewhat more active position. These factors balance each other out so that chances must be judged as about equal. This evaluation does not, however, prevent White from losing in short order:

27 b3

Black had the positional threat 27 ... Rc4 as it is clearly not in White's interest to strengthen Black's pawn formation with 28 Nxd5 cxd5. The text is perfectly O.K., though the resulting queenside weakening could have been avoided by the modest 27 Be1.

27 ... Bh6!

Black logically aims to either activate or exchange off his presently passive bishop.

28 Bxh6?!

Starting with this move, White dreams of attacking Black's king. The meager amount of material remaining does not allow the fulfillment of this dream. White in fact has slightly the worse position: the less effective minor piece and weakened queenside. As Regan pointed out after the game, equality could have been retained after 28 Nxd5! Rxd5 29 Bc3.

28 ...   Nxb4
29 c4   Ra5
30 h4?

Again in the spirit of an attack, but at the excessive cost of weakening the g4 square. As will be soon seen, Black's knight finds a marvelous home there. After the modest and correct 30 h3 White's disadvantage would be minor.

30 ...   Ra1+
31 Kh2   Nd3
32 Rd2   e4
33 Re2   Kf7!

Playable was 33 ... f5. Instead Black prefers to activate his king, realizing that the coming exchange of pawns serves to strengthen the superiority of his knight.

34 Rxe4   Nxf2
35 Rf4

just chases the knight to greener pastures. The centralizing 35 Rd4 was a shade better.

35 . . .	Nd3
36 Rd4	Ne5
37 Bf4	Ng4+
38 Kh3?!	

Allowing the king to be caught on the edge of the board is equivalent to suicide. After the obvious 38 Kg3, White would be a tempo ahead of the game and Black would have to work much harder for his point.

38 . . .	h5!
39 Rd7+?!	

Now White chases Black's king to where it wants to go. The rational move still was 39 Kg3.

39 . . .	Ke6
40 Rc7	Kf5
41 Bh2	

The kind of move one sometimes plays after he notes that sensible looking moves all fail, e.g. 41 g3 leads to mate after 41 . . . Ra2, while 41 Kg3 loses to 41 . . . Rb1! 42 Rb7 Rd1! (threatening 43 . . . Rd3+ with mate to follow) 43 Kf3 Rf1+ and 44 . . . Rxf4.

41 . . .	Rh1

winning the "inferior" bishop and with it the game.

42 Rxc6	Nxh2
43 Kg3	Ng4
44 Rc5+	Ke4
White resigns	

Considerably more complicated is the next example, Diagram 20, K.

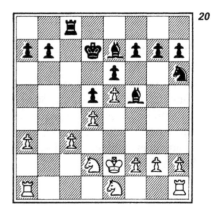

Regan–E. Mednis, 1978 US Championship after Black's 21st move. What is the state of affairs? White is ahead a whole exchange, but is burdened by a chronically backward and weak c-pawn, a somewhat weak a-pawn and an "undeveloped" knight on e1. Black has the two bishops and an overall sound position. Who is better? The subsequent course of the game shows this position to be dynamically equal. That's fine in hindsight, the reader can say, but how can we tell ahead of time Diagram 20 is fully satisfactory for Black? Foresight is, of course, much harder than hindsight, and there is little 100% certainty in chess. I wasn't therefore 100% certain that Black is fine, but I felt reasonably confident fundamentally, and even more confident from a practical aspect. A lot of such "feeling" comes from experience, yet the objective elements for evaluating the position are also clearly present. For instance, Black's position is "nice", the two bishops are a potential power and White will have to play the retreating 22 Nb1 to protect the c-pawn. As soon as Black can get his knight into the game, he will be ready to start bothering White. On the other hand, it is not to be seen where White's play will come from—on the contrary, any overextension by White could allow Black's bishops to develop devastating power. Though the future is decidedly uncertain, Black has no reason to be fearful of it:

22 Nb1   b6

By protecting the b-pawn, Black theatens 23 . . . Bxb1 24 Rxb1 Rxc3.

23 Nd3   f6!

attacking the center and allowing for the redeployment of the knight via f7. In spite of being the exchange down, Black plays methodically, no matter that this may appear slow. Of course now 24 exf6? gxf6 would give Black excellent central presence as well as potential play along the g-file and a marvelous spot for his knight on d6. The immediate 24 Rc1 would give Black the option for active play with 24 . . . Bxd3+ 25 Kxd3 fxe5 26 dxe5 Ng4. Thus White with his next move defends f2, thereby removing any potential threats to it.

24 Ra2   Nf7
25 f4   fxe5
26 Nxe5+

Not an obvious decision to make, as after the exchange of knights Black's bishops could be expected to obtain more scope. Yet the alternatives are even less attractive: 25 dxe5 yields additional central space to Black, while 26 fxe5 Ng5 allows Black's knight to become active.

26 . . .   Nxe5
27 fxe5

After 27 dxe5?! Black could well decide to play 27 . . . Bxb1 28 Rxb1 Rxc3 since his d-pawn is then passed.

27 . . .   Bg5!

The theme of Black's prospects is the utilization of the two bishops in a fairly open position to both bother White's king and keep the various weak pawns under attack. Therefore, inconsistent would be an immediate 27 . . . Bxb1?! 28 Rxb1 Rxc3. By winning back a pawn, Black has decreased his material disadvantage to a minimum, yet the terms of the exchange are not attractive. Black has had to part with the bishop pair, White is rid of an inactive knight, the pawn that is won is chronically weak anyway and, most important, Black then lacks any meaningful active plan. The above exchange should of course always be kept in mind, but only executed when there is a concrete, favorable follow-up.

Dangerous is 30 g4?! Bg6 and White has seriously weakened his kingside. Black can try to exploit it two ways: (1) by opening up the position further starting with . . . h5 or (2) by a properly timed . . . Bxb1, as after capturing the c-pawn, Black's rook will be in a position to go after White's kingside. White's king now "threatens" to flee to relative safety with 31 Kc2; therefore . . .

30 . . .	Bg6+
31 Ke2	Bh5+
32 Kd3	Draw

Dynamic equilibrium exists.

28 h3	Bg6!
29 Rf1	Bh5+!
30 Kd3!	

4

Characteristic Endgame Errors

How to draw inferior and win superior endgames will be discussed in some detail later on. Nevertheless, it seems appropriate now to consider the important field of errors. The most important types of errors are presented below.

1. Blunders (tragic and/or inexplicable errors)

Some errors must be called both tragic and inexplicable. For tragedy in real professional life there is little that can beat the course of play from Diagram 21, L. Alburt – R. Dzindzihashvili, Lone Pine 1980, after Black's 43rd move. It is the last round and the winner will pocket $15,000; a draw is worth $10,670 for each; the loser will wind up with $3940. White is a pawn up, while having three connected passed pawns. With two moves to go until the time control at move 45, is there a simpler way to negate the threat on the knight than by playing 44 Nxb7? After the forced 44 . . . Kxb7, White plays the obvious 45 h4, is out of time trouble and can look forward to a simple enough queening of the h-pawn and the $15,000. Yet the actual course of the game is quite different:

44 Qd8?   Qe5+!

Perhaps White had only considered 44 . . . Qd5? 45 Nxb7! Qxb7. Even then it must be recognized that for queening the h-pawn White's queen stands better on g5 than d8.

45 g3   Qe2!

The time control is over, but Black's attack on f2 guarantees him the draw. White should now play 46 Nxb7, safeguarding the $10,670.

46 Qf8??   Bf3!

How the picture has changed! The mate threat can only be parried by losing the knight. Black collected the $15,000 as follows:

47	Qf7+	Kb8
48	Qg8+	Kc7
49	Ne8+	Kc6
50	Qg6+	Kb5
51	Qb1+	Ka4
52	Kg1	Qxe8
53	Qa2+	Kb5
54	c4+	Kc6
55	Qa4+	b5
56	Qxa6+	Kc7
57	Qa5+	Kb7
58	cxb5	Qg6!
59	Kh2	c4
60	Qa3	Bd5
61	h4	Qf6
62	f4	c3
63	Qc5	Qe6!
64	f5	Qe2+
65	Kh3	Bg2+
66	Kh2	Bf3+
White resigns		

As far as pure chess tragedy is concerned, what happened at Lone Pine two years earlier is even worse. Diagram 22 shows J. Mestel – W. Browne, Lone Pine 1978, after

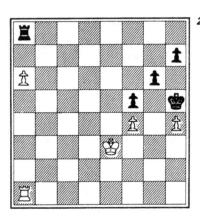

22

White's 47th move. Even though the time control has been reached, the players are oblivious of it and are still blitzing away. The a-pawn can be considered to give White the edge, but there is no way to take advantage of this, since if White's king heads for the queenside, Black's active king ensures full counterplay on the kingside. The simplest way to demonstrate this is 47 . . . Kg4!, as subsequently pointed out by Browne himself. Yet in the game he saw a "loose pawn", which, however, turned out to be an extremely poisonous one:

47 . . .   Kxh4??
48 Kf3!
Black resigns

Next move comes 49 Rh1 MATE!

Next worse to losing one's king is losing one's queen. Look how it's done from Diagram 23, S. Reshevsky – A. Belyavsky,

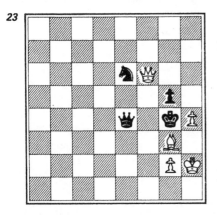

Vilnius 1978, after White's 67th move. True that White is a pawn up, but after some sensible move by Black—such as 67 . . . Qf5— White's winning chances are infinitesimal. But:

67 . . .   gxh4??
68 Qxh4+   Kf5
69 Qh7+
Black resigns

70 Qxe4 comes next.

Is there something we can do to prevent such blundering? Yes, of course. The most important precaution is to take some time before we play our move. The single greatest cause of blunders is extreme time pressure, because if you have no time to think, your chances for a blunder increase dramatically. Therefore avoid the kind of time pressure where only seconds are available for each move. The second "helpful hint" is to develop an attitude of carefulness. To foreclose the pain of being hit by lightning from above, try to make sure that you see the thundershowers possible in the position.

2. Making an automatic move

Since chess is for the thinking person, anything which short-circuits thinking is a potential problem. High on the list of problems is that of the "automatic move". You no doubt have experienced the feeling where just a quick glance at the position tells you that "*xyz* must be the right move". Well, please look again and make sure that it is actually so. Some moves may look automatic alright, but turn out to be quite wrong. The following two examples will drill this point home.

Diagram 24 shows the position in E. Mednis – R. Fischer, 1963/64 US Championship, after Black's 41st move. Earlier I had missed a win and then in time pressure a forced draw. But now even though I had another hour available to think, I quickly played:

24

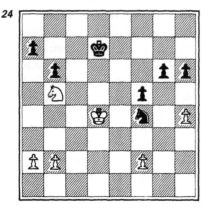

42 Nxa7??

I didn't even bother concentrating on this move, since, obviously, "a loose pawn must be captured". But of course there is no rational chess explanation for such an attitude. White takes off an unimportant pawn far from the scene of action, while forgetting about everything else! Just a bit of *thinking* would have shown that the active 42 Ke5! was in order, with a likely draw. Then 42 . . . Ng2 is harmless because of 43 h5 gxh5 44 Kxf5 and 42 . . . Nd3+ 43 Kf6 Nxf2 44 Kxg6 f4 45 Nd4 also looks quite safe for White.

| 42 . . . | Ng2 |
| 43 Ke5?! | |

Giving Black two connected passed pawns turns out to be quite hopeless. Therefore a better practi-

cal try is 43 h5 gxh5 44 Kd3! h4 45 Ke2 h3 46 Kf1, even though White's prospects remain bleak after 46 . . . Nh4 47 Kg1 Nf3+.

In the game, Black effectively neutralizes White's extra pawn on the queenside, while maximizing his chances on the kingside and wins very convincingly:

43 . . .	Nxh4
44 Kf4	g5+
45 Kg3	Ng6
46 a4	f4+
47 Kg2	g4
48 Nb5	Ne5!
49 Nc3	Ke6!
50 b4	Nc6!
51 f3?!	h5
52 b5	Ne5!
53 fxg4	hxg4
54 Kf2	Nd3+
55 Ke2	Nc5!
56 Kf1	Kf5
57 Kg2	Ke5
58 Kf2	Nd3+
59 Ke2	g3!
60 Kf3	Ne1+
61 Ke2	g2
62 Kf2	f3
White resigns	

What White does from Diagram 25, S. Gligoric – B. Larsen, Portoroz/Ljubljana 1977, after Black's 48th move is no more excusable. Black here has various obvious advantages: his king can assist

25

in the passed pawn's advance and is more active than White's king, Black's passed pawn is the more advanced one, White's king is cut off on the first rank. Nevertheless, material is severely reduced and equal and White can defend well enough, since Black's rook at the moment is clumsily placed in front of his own pawn:

49 Rd2!	Rb1+
50 Kf2??	

The psychological explanation for this error is that for many moves White had labored under the handicap of having his king contained to the first rank. So on the first chance to leave it, White in a knee-jerk reaction does so. But in chess terms the move is very wanting. The real chess point of White's previous

move surely was not to liberate the king by a bit, since clearly Black's K + b-pawn is much more of a force than White's K + g-pawn. No, the perceptive idea behind 49 Rd2! was to keep bothering Black's rook with 50 Rd1!, since if the rook goes to b3 or b4 it will be in the way of the b-pawn. After 50 Rd1! White can draw, but now the black rook remains active and White loses.

50 ...	b4
51 Kf3	b3
52 Ke4	Rg1!
53 Kxe5	Kc3
54 Rf2	b2
55 Rxb2	Kxb2
56 e4	Kc3
57 Kd6	Rd1+!

The key here and in the further play is to make sure that Black's rook and king can work as a team in preventing the advance of White's furthest passed pawn—here the e-pawn.

58 Ke6	Kd4!
59 g4	Rg1!
60 e5	Ke4!
61 Kf6	Rf1+!
62 Ke6	Ra1!
63 Kf6	Ra6+
64 e6	Kd5
65 g5	Rxe6+
White resigns	

3. Taking things too easily in a won position

Annotators are used to comments such as "from now on the game plays itself" or "the rest is elementary". Don't you believe this, and especially not if it is your game that is being played! A very common error in amateur games is taking things too easily in a won position. Even grandmasters are periodically afflicted by this error disease. Witness what happens from Diagram 26, R. Vaganian – E. Vasyukov, 1974 USSR Championship, after Black's 56th move. It is

easy enough to see that the combination of c- and e-pawns will cost Black his rook. However, White does have to ensure that his g-pawn is not lost. Therefore, unsatisfactory is the immediate 57 c8=Q? Rxc8 58 e8=Q Rxe8 59 Rxe8 be-

cause after 59 . . . Nh3! 60 Re5 Kg6 Black wins White's last pawn for a theoretical draw.

However, from the diagram easily winning is 57 Rc5!, e.g. 57 . . . Rc8 58 Rb5! Ng6 59 e8=Q! Rxe8 60 Rb8—a rather basic maneuver for achieving pawn promotion. But under the illusion that "everything wins", White plays the careless . . .

57 Ke3??

The move does have the strategic point that after 57 . . . Ng6? 58 c8=Q Rxc8 59 e8=Q Rxe8 60 Rxe8 White's g-pawn is safe. And obviously the "tactical" 57 . . . Rxe7? 58 Rxe7 Nd5+ isn't feasible because 58 Rxe7 is with *check*. Yet Black can reverse the move order in this line!

57 . . .	Nd5+!!
58 Kd4	

A painful move to have to play, but there are no practical winning chances at all after 58 Rxd5 Rxe7+ 59 Kf4 Rxc7.

58 . . .	Nxc7
59 Kc5	Ra8
60 Kc6	Ne8
Draw	

White's c-pawn has gone lost for nothing, and the best that White can do is to capture the knight for the e-pawn—which is still quite insufficient for the win.

4. Playing for a win without a valid reason

A different category of errors results from insisting in playing for a win when there are objectively no rational winning chances. As an introduction to this theme, let us follow the play from Diagram 27, M. Quinteros – T. Weinberger,

27

Cleveland 1975, after White's 51st move. During the previous play Black has been handicapped by having his knight on the corner of the board, but now he spies a creative opportunity to get it back into the game.

51 . . .	Nc7!!
52 Qxc7	

leads by force to perpetual check. Yet with Black's knight back, other methods also do not promise a win, e.g. 52 Bb7 Ne8 or 52 Bd4+ Kf8! (Not 52 . . . Bf6? 53 Bxf6+ Kxf6 54 Qc3+!, winning).

52 . . .	Qxd5+
53 Kf1	Qd3+!
54 Ke1	

If 54 Kg1, 54 . . . Qd1+ etc.

54 . . .	Bf6

With the obvious threat 55 . . . Bc3+, so that White must free f2 for his king.

55 Bb6	Bc3+
56 Kf2	Qd2+
57 Kf3	Qd1+!
58 Ke3	Qd2+
59 Ke4	

By forcing . . . d5, White takes that square away from Black's queen. But it makes no difference, since Black still has perpetual check.

59 . . .	d5+
60 Kf3	Qd1+
61 Kg2	Qe2+

Since 62 Bf2? fails to 62 . . . Bd4, White has nothing better than to acquiesce to the perpetual check after 62 Kg1 Qe1+ etc.

62 Kh3??

The Argentine grandmaster wants to make sure that Black sees the perpetual check after 62 . . . Qh5+ 63 Kg2 Qe2+.

62 . . .   Qf1+!!

But Black "sees" much more!

63 Kg4   h5+
White resigns

He gets mated after both 64 Kg5 Bf6 and 64 Kh4 Bf6.
Diagram 28, I. Farago – L. Vogt, Kecskemet 1977, after Black's 31st

move, shows what befalls those who only think of themselves. For some time White has had the material advantage of two minor pieces for a rook, but his uncertain play has

allowed Black to reach the diagramed position. Black's active rook plus kingside pawns ensure him the draw, yet White can't accept this for psychological reasons and plays the "winning" . . .

32 Nf7+??

In fact, White had nothing better than 32 Nb7+ Kc7 33 Nc5, after which the most sensible continuation is 33 . . . Rg2+ 34 Kh1 Rf2 35 Kg1 Rg2+ with a draw. After the text move White does win the e-pawn, yet after . . .

32 . . .   Kc5
White resigns

. . . he loses the game! Black's king has been liberated and suddenly White is defenseless. For instance, 33 Nxe5 Kd4 34 f4 Ke3 and there is nothing to be done about 35 . . . Rb1 check and mate.

A sister case to the above is where a player, after misplaying a won endgame, plods on almost as if by inertia until the errors come and come. This is illustrated from Diagram 29, E. Geller – I. Dorfman, 1978 USSR Zonal (Lvov), after Black's 40th move. Despite some earlier inaccuracies, White's position is still won because he can win Black's a-pawn and then promote his own. Play continued:

29

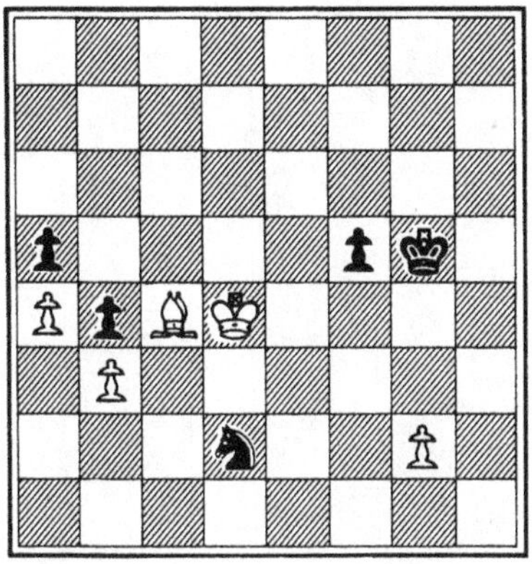

42 ...	Nf1
43 Kc4	Ne3+
44 Kb5	Nxg2
45 Kxa5	Ke5
46 Kxb4	Kd6
47 Kb5??	

Losing a tempo here spoils all of the previous effort. Utilizing the principle "passed pawns must be pushed", correct and winning is 47 a5!

41 Bg8!

By placing the bishop away from any knight forks and captures, White frees the king for its advance.

41 ...	Kf4
42 Kd3!	

Some sophistication is required here. After the obvious 42 Kc5?, Black has the following drawing line, as given by Geller: 42 ... Ke3! 43 Kb5 Kd4! 44 Kxa5 Kc3 45 Kb6 Nxb3! 46 a5 Nxa5! and Black will be able to exchange off White's last pawn.
After the text move, Black's knight must give ground. 42 ... Ne4 loses to 43 Kc4 Nf6 44 Be6 Ke5 45 Bxf5! Kxf5 46 Kb5 Nd5 47 Kxa5 Ke5 48 Kb5 Kd4 49 a5 Kc3 50 Kc6! (Geller).

47 ...	f4!
48 Bc4	f3
49 Kb6	Ne3
50 Bd3	Nd5+
51 Kb7	Kc5!

Now that Black's king can get at the b-pawn, the position is drawn.

52 a5	f2
53 Bf1	

Simplest is 53 a6 Nb4 54 Bf1 Nxa6 55 Kxa6 Kb4.

53 ...	Nb4
54 Bc4??	

Pointless and bad. The bishop accomplishes nothing on c4 and is vulnerable there. But White can't get himself to acquiesce to the draw after 54 a6 Nxa6 etc.

54 ...	Nc6!
55 a6??	

Allowing the following check is unforgivable. There was nothing better than giving up both of the queenside pawns and rushing to draw on the kingside after 55 Bf1 Nxa5+ 56 Kc7 Nxb3 57 Kd7.

55 . . .	Na5+
56 Kb8	Nxc4
57 bxc4	f1=Q
58 a7	Qf8+
59 Kb7	Qe7+
60 Kb8	Kb6
White resigns	

If you don't want to be hurt by these kinds of errors, try to remain as objective as possible. Greatest chess successes come to those who always try to search for the truth. There are times when a position cannot be won. Accept this as a fact of life. And there almost always is a tomorrow!

5. Underestimating power of passed pawns

As already pointed out earlier, the endgame is the arena where the passed pawn(s) can develop tremendous power. Many endgame errors result from underestimating this power. A drastic illustration is from Diagram 30, N. Gaprindashvili – U. Andersson, Dortmund 1978,

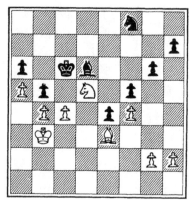

after Black's 33rd move. The position looks drawish, since White's queenside advantage is balanced by Black's edge on the kingside. Black, however, is in severe time trouble, so that White tries a "bit of tactics":

| 34 cxb5+! | Kxd5?? |

Hallucination or wishful thinking? Did Black really "think" that White had left the knight hanging? Correct is the safe 34 . . . Kxb5! 35 Nc3+ Kc6 36 Kc4 Ne6! 37 g3 Nc7 with equality.

| 35 bxa6 | Ne6 |

The pawns also roll forward after 35 . . . Kc6 36 b5+! Kc7 37 b6+ Kc6 38 a7 Kb7 39 a6+.

36 a7	Nc7
37 b5!	
Black resigns	

The conclusion would be 37 . . . Na8 38 b6 Kc6 39 a6! and there is nothing to be done about the coming 40 b7.

In endgames where both sides have passed pawns, the most prevelant error is sloppiness in calculation. Because such positions offer fantastic chances for both, it is absolutely imperative to try to calculate everything as accurately as possible. So very often one tempo is the difference between complete success and abject failure. There is no better example of this than from Diagram 31, S. Tarrasch – Emanuel Lasker, Hastings 1895, after Black's

40th move. Material is even, so clearly the decisive factor must be the passed pawns. Whose are stronger?

41 Kf5??

It was imperative to eliminate Black's pawn with 41 Nxc3!. Best play then is 41 . . . Kxc3 42 Kf5! b5! 43 g5 Bxg5! 44 Kxg5 Kb2 45 h4 Kxa2 46 h5 b4 47 h6 b3 48 h7 b2 49 h8=Q b1=Q. Black has some winning chances, but the endgame probably is drawn.

41 . . .   Kd3??

Losing a crucial tempo changes a won position into a lost one. Black wins after 41 . . . c2!, as shown in the following analysis by Pillsbury: 42 g5 Bxg5! 43 Kxg5 Kd3 44 Nc1+ Kd2 45 Nb3+ Kd1 46 Kf5 (There is nothing better) 46 . . . a5 47 a4 b5! 48 axb5 a4 49 b6 (Or 49 Nc1 Kxc1 50 b6 a3 51 b7 a2 52 b8=Q a1=Q) 49 . . . axb3 50 b7 b2 51 b8=Q c1=Q, with a won Q + P ending.

42 Nxc3!   Kxc3
43 g5   Bb6

After the "necessary" 43 . . . Bxg5 Black is a tempo behind the line given in the note to White's 41st move and therefore loses.

44 h4   Bd4
45 h5   b5
46 h6   b4
47 g6   a5
48 g7   a4
49 g8=Q
Black resigns

This endgame—played three rounds before the end—determined the ultimate top placings. Had Lasker won it, he would have tied for first with Pillsbury, rather than finishing in third place.

5

Exchange of Major Pieces in Endgames: When and Why

You have an endgame involving queens. Under what circumstances should you exchange your queen? When should you retain it? Similar questions arise for endgames where the rook is the major piece.

With the help of the examples below, I shall try to give clear guidelines for the required decision making. Queen exchanges will be covered first, and, as will be seen, the same principles will also apply for rook exchanges.

The most basic need always is to remain objective. Everyone really wants to be able to judge a position correctly. Human frailty being what it is, this is not to be achieved every time. But there is no excuse for not even *trying*. A perfect example here is Diagram 32, L. Psakhis – T. Petrosian, USSR 1982, after Black's 27th move. Black has just played 27 . . . Qa8 challenging White's control of the a-file. There simply is nothing else for White do to than to accept dead-eye endgame

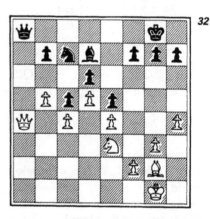

32

equality with 28 Qxa8. But instead White plays:

28 Qd1?

How can it ever be right to hand over control of the a-file to Black *for nothing*?

28 . . .	Ne8
29 Kh2	Nf6
30 Qf3	h5?!

This slight weakening of the king-side allows White sufficient attack-

35

ing chances for the draw. As Petrosian himself has suggested, correct is 30 . . . Qd8! 31 Bh3 Bxh3 32 Kxh3 g6 33 Kg2 Kg7. With the kingside then safe, Black follows up with 34 . . . Qa5 and keeps the advantage.

31	Bh3	Bxh3
32	Kxh3	Qa1
33	Kg2	Qb1
34	Nf5!	Nxe4
35	Ne7+	Kf8
36	Ng6+	Kg8

After 36 . . . Ke8, 37 Qf5! secures a draw by perpetual check.

37 Ne7+   Draw

Since the queen is such a powerhouse, the first consideration should always be: how much damage can it do? In other words, is my queen well placed for the attack? Or is my opponent's queen the major threat? Such an evaluation will usually lead us to the correct decision. Let us now consider Diagram 33, V. Korchnoi – U. Andersson, Wijk aan Zee 1983, after Black's 48th move. The blocked pawn formation makes Black's knight an agile attacker. Moreover, both bases of White's pawn chains — at c4 and f3 — are vulnerable to attack by Black's bishop. In addition, Black threatens a kingside attack via Ng6, Nf4 and

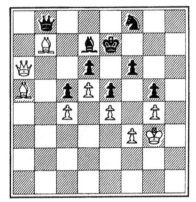

33

Qh8. However, the awesome position of White's queen keeps the chances fully in balance. But for this active play is necessary.

Logical, therefore, is 49 Bc6! and if 49 . . . Bc8, 50 Qb5!. Then 50 . . . Qxb5?! 51 cxb5! is good for White and 50 . . . Qa7 51 Be8! also keeps White's forces active. If Black immediately goes for the attack with 49 . . . Ng6!? 50 Bxd7 Qb1!?, White saves himself by 51 Bd8+!!: 51 . . . Kxd7 (Of course not 51 . . . Kxd8?? 52 Qc8+ Ke7 53 Qe8 Mate. And after 51 . . . Kf7 White has 52 Be8+!! Kxe8 53 Qc6+ Kf7 54 Qd7+ Kg8 55 Qe6+ Kh7 56 Qf7+ Kh6 57 Qxf6! and since Black's knight is pinned White is safe.) 52 Qc6+ Kxd8 53 Qxd6+ Ke8 (53 . . . Kc8 54 Qe6+ leads to a loss of Black's knight) 54 Qe6+ Ne7 55 d6 and Black must take perpetual check. It is true, of course, that to visualize all of this from the starting position is very difficult. Yet the principle remains clear: White must look for counter-play from his active queen!

| 49 Qa8?? | Qxa8 |
| 50 Bxa8 | Ba4 |

Now White has nothing but weaknesses and is hopelessly lost.

51 Bc6	Bd1
52 Bd2	Ng6
53 Be3	Nh4
54 f4	exf4+
55 Bxf4	gxf4+
56 Kxh4	Bc2
57 Kh3	Bxe4
58 Ba4	Kf7
59 Bd1	Bd3
White resigns	

In inferior positions, even when they are less complicated than the previous example, it is usually imperative to keep the queen so that chances for counterplay exist. Diagram 34, Grün – K. Darga, West Germany 1982, after White's 35th move, offers a typical example. White has three pawns for the piece and the advantage because his pawns are healthy and Black's bishop has little chance of attacking White's pawns. White's winning attempts will consist of creating a passed pawn on the queenside and also judiciously using the king + kingside pawns on the kingside.

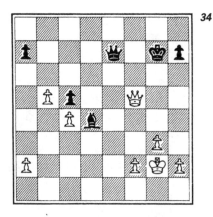

34

Whatever chances Black has must come from having the potential power of his queen. A logical move, therefore, now is 35 . . . Qe2!?. But instead Black plays:

35 . . .   Qf7??

The above discussion demonstrated why keeping the queens on is required. To voluntarily offer the exchange is equivalent to suicide.

36 Qxf7+!	Kxf7
37 f4	Ke6
38 Kf3	

White has sound pawn majorities on both sides, while Black's bishop is offensively impotent. This endgame is 100% won for White.

38 . . .	Bc3
39 g4!	Be1
40 Ke4	h6

41 h3	Bg3
42 a4!	Be1
43 g5!	h5

Or 43 . . . hxg5 44 fxg5 Kf7 (44 . . . Bh4 45 a5 Bxg5 46 b6 axb6 47 a6) 45 Kd5 and White's king penetrates and wins. Notice how, after the exchange of queens, White's king starts ruling the board.

44 f5+	Kd6
45 g6	Bc3
46 a5!	

Black resigns

In the last two examples we looked at the position with the eyes of the defender. If we are trying to win a superior position then we simply switch our thinking around. In other words, if the enemy queen is a potentially dangerous attacker, try to eliminate this counterplay by exchanging it off. The other important case is where the enemy queen as a defender is able to just defend all of the vulnerable points. In general, the queen because of its strength can function both as a marvelous attacker and defender. The correct strategy then becomes to exchange off the defensive queen so that the enemy position then lacks defensive means. This is beautifully demonstrated from Diagram 35, U. Andersson – B. Gulko, Biel Interzonal 1976, after Black's 21st move. Black's c-pawn is under very strong pressure and Black's b- and d-pawns can also become very vulnerable. Moreover, if the d-pawn is undermined, then the e-pawn most likely will be lost. Also the a5 and b6 squares are weak and c5 can also become weak if the d-pawn is forced to move. The only thread that holds all of these weaknesses together is the queen. Therefore:

| 22 Qa4!! | Qxa4 |
| 23 Nxa4 | |

Black had hardly any choice but to exchange. However, White's minor pieces are now ready to take over Black's queenside. Rather bleak for Black now is 23 . . . cxb5 24 cxb5 Bd7 25 Nc3 Nd4 26 Nc4. Yet the game continuation is no better.

23 . . .	Bd7
24 Nb6!	Be8
25 bxc6!	Bxc6

After 25 . . . bxc6 White breaks up Black's pawn formation with 26 c5!.

26 Nb3!

The knight calmly heads for the b-pawn, starting with 27 Na5. Since there is no defense to this, Black tries an abortive central action which is easily refuted.

26 . . .	e4
27 Bxf6	Bxf6
28 Bxe4	Nd4
29 Bxc6!	bxc6
30 Nxd4	Bxd4
31 Nc8	Bc5
32 Ne7+	
Black resigns	

As an attacker, the rook is very powerful, truly being a major piece. Those playing for the win from a superior position must always be on guard from potential counterplay by the enemy rook. In such situations, playing to exchange off the enemy rook becomes an integral part of successful strategy. A good example is from Diagram 36, G. Agzamov – V. Kupreichik, Erevan 1982, after Black's 25th move. Black's queenside pawns are mangled, and since he has no compensation for this, White clearly has the superior chances. However, it is difficult for White to exploit his superiority since Black's rook is

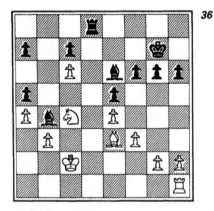

36

well placed on the d-file. For instance, 26 Bxa7? allows 26 . . . Bxc4 27 bxc4 Rd2+. Noting also that White's rook has little to do at present makes it easy to come up with White's correct plan:

26 Rd1! Rxd1

Unattractive, of course, but if the rook moves away, then it is White's rook which controls the open d-file.

27 Kxd1	a6
28 Ba7!	Kf8
29 Bb8	Bd6

Already something has to give on the queenside, as 29 . . . Bxc4 30 bxc4 Bd6 is met by 31 c5.

30 Kc2	Ke7
31 Nxa5	f5

Now instead of the game's 32 h3?! which both cost a tempo and weakened the kingside (though White still won in 40 after Black errors), Agzamov gives the following convincing line:

32 Kc3!	fxe4
33 fxe4	Bg4
34 Nc4	Be2
35 b4	

White has a winning position. He is up a very healthy pawn and even threatens to trap Black's queen's bishop with 36 Ne3, e.g. 35 . . . Bf1?! 36 Ne3 Be2 37 Kd2 Bh5 38 g4 Bxb4+ 39 Ke2.

Whenever your opponent's rook(s) are more active than yours, give a high priority to trying to exchange them off. This is generally a very useful strategy in drawing inferior endgames. Look now at Diagram 37, Gavrikov – V. Malanyuk, USSR 1982, after Black's 19th move. White's extra

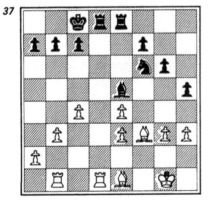

pawn is a nothing, since Black can get back the e4 pawn at his own convenience. What is significant is that all of Black's four pieces are placed very actively, with both rooks on the central files. White should now be concerned with trying to neutralize Black's pressure. In the game White in a burst of unjustified optimism played 20 b4? but after 20 . . . Rd6! (threatening both 21 . . . Rde6 and 21 . . . Ra6) 21 Rxd6 Bxd6 22 c5 Bf8 Black recaptured the pawn on e4 while keeping a strong initiative and won on move 46. The correct strategy is:

20 Rxd8+!	Rxd8
21 Rd1!	Rxd1
22 Bxd1	Nxe4
23 Kg2	
with equality.	

With the rooks off, White can protect the rest of his weak points with no difficulty. Moreover, he can go for further simplification with 24 g4.

But in trying to hold a position where your weaknesses cannot be cured, the key strategy must be counterplay. Make your rook(s) active and keep it active! A typical situation is shown in Diagram 38, J. Timman – B. Larsen, Las Palmas Interzonal 1982, after Black's 37th move. Despite the extra pawn, White is in some trouble, since Black's rooks and knight are well

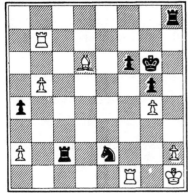

38

placed to both attack White's king and the queenside. Yet the three white pieces can fashion an attack on Black's somewhat loose king if White is determined enough. But short on time he runs scared and plays:

38 Rb8?

Now Black will devour White's queenside and have a riskless winning position. As Timman subsequently pointed out, correct is the active 38 Rb6!, threatening 39 Be5. Black has nothing better than 38 . . . Nf4 and after 39 Bxf4 gxf4 40 Rxf4 Rhxh2+ 41 Kg1 Rxa2 there is no shortage of draws in the position but nothing more.

38 . . .	Rxb8
39 Bxb8	Rxa2
40 Bd6	Rb2
41 Be7	Nf4

42 h4	Rxb5
43 hxg5	hxg5

With a healthy pawn advantage Black should win. (However, because of a subsequent blunder Black was forced to trade the a-pawn for White's g-pawn and the game ended in a draw on move 63.)

Compared to its offensive powers, as a defender the rook is somewhat clumsy. But, of course, it still is a defender. Therefore, often an effective technique for the stronger side is to exchange off the enemy rook. This is an obvious strategy when the rook is the bastion that holds back the decisive advance of a passed pawn. The more sophisticated application of the exchanging strategy occurs when there are serious weaknesses in the enemy camp but the rook is just able to cover them. A typical example is shown in Diagram 39,

39

A. Groszpeter – L. Popov, Plovdiv 1982, after White's 34th move. Black has a clear advantage because of the following factors: White's e-pawn is weak, Black's d-pawn is passed, White's knight is out on a limb, Black's bishops have marvelous scope. The glue that holds White's position together is his rook. Therefore Black plays:

34 . . .   Ra1!
35 Rxa1

Not desirable, but 35 Rd3 leaves Black's rook the lord of the first rank with a devastating pin.

35 . . .   Bxa1
36 f4   Bd5!

In the game Black played 36 . . . Kg7 37 Bc4 d5 and also won. However, the bishop pair's strength is demonstrated even better in the text line as given by Popov.

37 Nc7   Bb3
38 Bb5   Bd4+
39 Kf1   Bb6
40 Na8   Ba5
Black wins

White knight is stalemated, Black wins the e-pawn and his bishops still sweep the board.

A more conventional exchanging maneuver is initiated from Diagram 40, M. Chandler – Borik, West

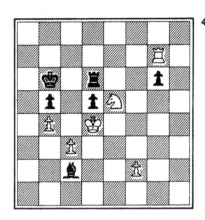

40

Germany 1982, after Black's 36th move. White obviously has the superior king and minor piece. But again Black's rook just holds things together. The correct plan by now should be clear to everyone.

37 Rd7!   Rxd7

This is hopeless. Yet after 37 . . . Rf6 38 f3! Bb3 39 Rg7! there is no defense to the dual threats of 40 Rxg6 and 40 Nd7+.

38 Nxd7+   Kc6
39 Nf6!   Bb3
40 Ke5!

With the king's penetration the end is near.

40 . . .	Bc4
41 Nh7!	Ba2
42 Nf8	Bb1
43 Ne6	Ba2
44 Nd4+	Kb6
45 Kd6!	Bc4
46 Ne6	Bb3
47 Nf4	g5

48 Nxd5+	Kb7
49 Nf6	Kb6
50 Nd7+	
Black resigns	

After 50 . . . Ka7 51 Kc5 Black's position offers not a whiff of a chance.

Part II

Winning Superior Endgames

One of the two major objectives of this book is to help the reader gain the maximum number of points from superior positions. The starting point in this section—the superior endgame—has already been reached from a superior middlegame. You, of course, want to win your superior endgame and absolutely never do you want to lose it. Winning superior endgames while drawing inferior ones in the greatest possible number of games will make you a most successful endgame player.

The observant reader may note that in the heading of this part I refer to *superior* endgames, but in the individual chapter titles use the expression *won* endgames. Well, in the actual playing of an advantageous endgame, the dividing line between a superior endgame becoming a won one is usually not at all sharp and often considerable post-game analysis is required to accurately determine the official "winning moment". But for practical players the difference is mostly academic. What is important to know is that the same principles apply to both *superior* and *won* endgames.

The single most important factor in winning superior/won endgames is having the proper attitude. Chapters 6 and 7 discuss what not to do, and then with this as a background the reader is fully ready to appreciate How to Win a Won Endgame in Chapter 8. The last two chapters cover two very important specific subjects: when is the knight or bishop the superior partner for a rook and the unique value of the passed rook pawn in knight endgames.

6

Drawing a Won Endgame

All of us have played over annotated games where at the start of a won endgame the annotator says something like: "The rest is a matter of technique. No further comments are required." Don't you believe this! No won endgames are won by default. Many things can go wrong on the way to the expected full point. It is true that such games are seldom published since they are messy to annotate. But they occur in real life often enough to be of considerable concern to all of us who want to win our won endgames.

To emphasize the damage that can be done to won positions, I shall use a negative approach, i.e. what *not* to do. In other words, if you do these things, you will not win. First we will look at cases where only half a loaf is lost—the won endgame is drawn.

Principle No. 1. You will not win a won endgame if you allow counterplay

Winning a won endgame should be looked upon as a continuous battle. In a real battle, you don't want to give the enemy a chance to attack any weak point in your line. After all, the line may not hold under the attack for either physical or psychological reasons. Your troops may panic in one spot and this panic could spread to the whole army.

Similar thinking prevails on the chessboard. In a won endgame, you control your destiny. You don't want anything to interfere with your plans for enlarging on your advantage. Any counterplay can cause you to lose your concentration and control. One inaccuracy often leads to another and soon there is no win at all. Therefore, never *voluntarily* allow any counterplay.

A good example to start our discussion with is Diagram 41, A. Yusupov – L. Psakhis, Erevan 1982, after Black's 28th move. At first glance the position may look complicated, but it is easy enough to split it into clear parts.

41

Black with two pawns for the exchange has a slight material advantage. Moreover, White's kingside is barren. However, Black cannot yet take advantage of this because, apart from the queen, the other three pieces are not yet in an attacking position. The queenside is all White's and this is the critical element because White can both expand his power there and nip Black's kingside dreams in the bud with:

29 Qc7!	Qxc7

There is no choice, since 29 . . . Qd3? loses the bishop after 30 Rcd1.

30 Rxc7	Nf6
31 Rd1	Bb5
32 b3!	e5!

Black's only hope for counterplay is his e-pawn, well supported by its rook.

33 a4	Be2
34 Rd2?	

This "safe" move actually is a serious inaccuracy for two specific reasons: (1) The e-pawn when it reaches e3 does it with gain of time and (2) Black can retain his rook. Remember that Black's counterplay must come from the combination of the e-pawn supported by his rook! Therefore, it is clear enough that correct and easily winning is 34 Rdc1! threatening 35 Rc8 and a rook exchange. The only way to prevent it is 34 . . . Kh7, and this fails to the simple 35 Rxf7.

34 . . .	Bh5
35 Bb7?	

This again is too ignorant of Black's potential counterplay and in fact spoils the win. White's task is already considerably harder than just a move earlier. Still, if he keeps in mind the principle of preventing/ minimizing counterplay, White can win with this line given by Yusupov: 35 Rdc2! Kh7! 36 Rc8 Re7! 37 R2c7 Re6 38 Rc6! Re7 39 Rxa6 e4 40 Rd6! e3 41 Rc1. White's pieces are placed very effectively, compared to the game continuation. Therefore the e-pawn can be neutralized and the passed queenside pawns will win.

35 . . .	Kh7!
36 Bxa6	e4
37 Be2	e3
38 Ra2	Nd5

Notice how Black has been able to mobilize his pieces with gain of time. His counterplay now is sufficient for the draw.

39 Rc4	Bxe2!
40 Rxe2	g5!
41 a5	

Yusupov suggests the immediate 41 Kg2 as a better winning try, but I'm not sure that it really matters.

41 . . .	Nf4
42 Rxf4	gxf4
43 Kg2	Re5!
Draw	

The passed pawn chains lead to dynamic balance and an inevitable equivalent dissolving of the chains. For instance, 44 b4 Re4 45 b5 Re5!.

Principle No. 2. You will not win a won endgame if you do not discipline yourself while playing it

The above principle is something like a catch-all for a number of items which deal with the need to always concentrate hard. The specific problem areas are as follows:

Taking things too easily: physically or psychologically

Not sitting down prior to moving, having already scored the point in one's mind, feeling that any move will be good enough to win are examples of what *not* to do.

Carelessness

As a result of overconfidence, not thinking hard enough prior to moving.

Giving up material

Don't give up material unless this is the only way to win. Too often unnecessary generosity finds you short of the necessary pawn(s).

Being fancy

The problems that occur from the first three items are excellently demonstrated in the play from Diagram 42, A. Miles – U. Andersson, London 1982, after Black's 28th move. White is an absolutely safe pawn up. Black has no compensation for this and there

is not a thing wrong with White's position. If ever there was a "matter of technique" endgame, this is it. Moreover, White is a world class grandmaster. But see what happens:

29 Kf2

By centralizing the king, White also prevents the incursion of Black's rook. Over the next ten moves or so White basically keeps

the status quo to reach the time control at move 40.

29 . . .	h5
30 Rd6	Rc7
31 Re6	Bb7
32 g3	Bc8
33 Rd6	Bd7
34 Bd5	Bg4
35 a3	Re7
36 Bc4	Rc7
37 Bf1	Kf7
38 h3	Ke7
39 Rd4	Be6
40 Bd3	Bxh3

This splits Black's pawns. Therefore, sounder is 40 . . . Kf7. However, Black wants to bring about some unbalancing of the position so that White has more of a chance to do something wrong.

41 Bxg6	Bg4
42 Rd5	Ke6
43 Be4?!	

The first serious misstep. White obviously thinks that the position will win itself, without any serious thinking on his part. By retreating the bishop, White gives up pressure against Black's vulnerable h-pawn, while gaining not a thing in return. Correct is the active 43 Rd8! penetrating into Black's position and threatening the immediate 44 Rh8. Then with White's R + B active, Black's h-pawn weak and White still with an extra pawn, decisive progress by White is not far away.

43 . . .   Rc8

preventing White's Rd8.

44 Ke3   Ke7
45 f5??

Truly a frightful, careless, sloppy, thoughtless move. White would never play it if he had actually done some *real thinking*. The scope of White's bishop is decreased, it is now more difficult to attack the h-pawn and the "payment" is in the reverse: instead of a sound pawn on f4, White has a vulnerable one on f5.

45 . . .   Rg8

Now Black even gets a bit of counterplay along the g-file.

46 Rd2   Bh3
47 Rh2??

Because of his 43rd and 45th moves, White has ruined his chances on the kingside. The best that he can do is to safeguard it with 47 Kf3 and then to start utilizing his pawn majority on the queenside. Instead, he commits the dual sins of carelessness and giving up material.

47 . . .   Rxg3+
48 Kf2   h4

White had only considered the "tricky" 48 . . . Rg4?? 49 Bf3 Rh4 50 Kg3 and White wins. The most simple text move was not noticed. Black now is even slightly better, since he will wind up with a passed f-pawn to balance White's extra queenside pawn. White does continue playing well enough to draw.

49 Rh1   Kd6
50 Rd1+   Ke5
51 Rd4   Bg4
52 a4!   a5
53 Bh1!   Bxf5
54 Rxh4   Rh3
55 Rxh3   Bxh3
56 Bc6   Kd6
57 Be4   Bd7
58 Bc2   Ke5
59 Ke3   Bg4
60 Bb3   Bf5
61 Bd1   Bb1
62 Bb3   f5
63 Bd1   f4+
64 Kf3   Be4+
65 Kf2   Kd5
66 Bb3+   Kc5
67 Ke2   Bc6
Draw

Never, never be fancy—when a simple line will do. Chess is just so inexaustible that much too often something surprising pops up in complicated variations. The resulting pain also hits those going for the world championship, as will be seen from Diagram 43, R. Hübner – L.

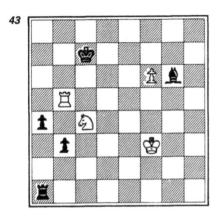

43

Portisch, Semi-final Candidates Match, 1980, Game 11, after Black's 42nd move. Here the game was adjourned with White sealing his move:

43 Ke2

The king must both remove himself from the f-file and head closer to the queenside to try to be of help in stopping the pawns. This move is by far the only logical one and was fully expected by Portisch and his seconds.

In the adjourned position Black has every right to expect a win: a pawn up and having far advanced connected passed pawns. For Portisch a win is crucial for the match, since he will then be only one game

behind and will have the white pieces in the final, 12th, game. But since no game is won without making moves, Black has to decide how to proceed from here. It is well known that when playing in events where he has seconds, Portisch does little adjournment analysis himself and prefers to spend the night soundly sleeping. And so it also happened here. In the morning his grandmaster seconds provided him with a variation which they guaranteed would win White's rook and with it the game. Portisch was not happy with it, but the seconds were very insistent that it won. When the game was resumed, he took another 18 minutes on the clock and finally played the recommended:

43 . . .   a3??

As Portisch tells of his unhappy experience, he was loath to give up his valuable b-pawn, but decided to trust his seconds. He had wanted to play the natural and logical 43 . . . Bf7!, but his seconds had spent no time analyzing it! That would have won easily, e.g. 44 Ne5 a3! 45 Nxf7 b2 46 Nd8! Re1+ 47 Kxe1 a2 48 f7 b1=Q+ 49 Rxb1 axb1=Q+ 50 Ke2 Qc2+ 51 Ke1 Qe4+ 52 Kd1 Qf3+ followed by 53 . . . Kxd8. Even more straightforward is the win after 44 Na5: 44 . . . Kd6 45 Kd2 Rf1! 46 Kc3

a3! 47 Nxb3 a2 followed by
48 ... Bxb3 and 49 ... a1=Q.
White's best try is 44 Nd2, but
Black still wins easily enough with the
thematic 44 ... a3! 45 Nxb3 Rb1!: 46
Kd2 a2 followed by 47 ... Bxb3 or 46
Ra5 Rxb3 47 Ra7+ Kb6! or 46 Nd4 a2
or 46 Rc5+ Kd6.

44 Rxb3	a2
45 Ra3	Bh5+
46 Kf2!	Rh1

and "Black wins the rook and the
game" was the conclusion of Portisch's helpers. The first part is true,
but not the second!

47 Ra7+!

Portisch's team had overlooked
(or, more accurately, had chosen to
pay no attention to) this check. It
turns out that Black's king has no
good square to go to: (a)
47 ... Kc6 48 Ne5+ Kb6 49 Rxa2
Rh2+ 50 Kg3 Rxa2 51 f7 Ra8 52
f8=Q Rxf8 53 Nd7+; (b)
47 ... Kd8 48 Ra8+ Kd7 49 Ra7+
Ke6 50 Ra6+ Kf7 (or 50 ... Kf5
51 Ne3+ Kg6 52 Rxa2 Rh2+ 53
Ng2) 51 Ne5+ Kg8 52 Ra8+ Kh7 53
f7 with a theoretical draw.

47 ...	Kb8

Therefore there is no choice, but
now the king is just too far away to
help stop the f-pawn. Thus White
draws even though he starts off a
whole rook down!

48 Rxa2	Rh2+
49 Kg3	Rxa2
50 Ne5	Kc7

Unfortunately 50 ... Ra6 does
not work because of 51 f7 Rf6 52
Nd7+.

51 f7	Ra8
52 Kh4	

with a gain of tempo!

52 ...	Rh8

Or 52 ... Kd6 53 Nc4+! Kd5 54
Kxh5 Kxc4 55 Kg6 and again
Black's king is one square too far
away.

53 Kg5	Kd6
54 Kf6!	
Draw	

Black cannot stop the drawing 55
Kg7, for instance, 54 ... Rc8 55
Kg7 Ke7 (55 ... Bxf7 56 Nxf7+ is
a clear theoretical and practical
draw) 56 Nc6+ followed by 57
f8=Q.

7

Losing a Won Endgame

It is bad enough if you draw a won endgame. But *losing* such an endgame is sure to bring about sleepless nights. How can such a tragedy occur? There are two basic causes. The first is a more extreme punishment of the type of errors and attitudes discussed earlier: taking things too easily, allowing counterplay, carelessness, blundering, etc. If the position is critical enough or the error severe enough, then in one move we can go from happiness to despair.

There is, however, also a truly fundamental reason why so many superior endgames are lost. I am stating this as follows: *You will lose a won endgame if you handle it contrary to the principles applicable to that type of endgame.* Almost every type of endgame has certain important principles particular to it. Whether it is rook + pawn(s), king + pawn(s), minor piece(s), queen + pawn(s), various types of passed pawns—each has its own peculiarities and needs. If, for instance, you

do not know anything about king + pawn endgames, should it really be surprising that you lose a superior ending to an opponent who is familiar with every trick and nuance within it?

The first, and relatively simple, example comes from Diagram 44, L. Bronstein – A. Yusupov, Lucerne Olympiad 1982, after Black's 32nd move. At first glance the position may appear both unclear and messy. For instance, both White and Black have many pawn

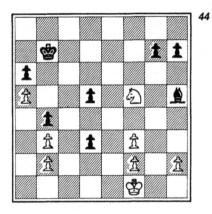

44

weaknesses. However, a relatively brief evaluation should be sufficient to determine that White has a vastly superior minor piece endgame. Why so? Because the nimble knight is capable of attacking and capturing every one of Black's weak six pawns, whereas Black's bishop can only attack two of White's pawns and both of these are relatively unimportant doubled pawns. Moreover, White's naturally centralized king will be marvelously positioned to both contain and menace Black's d-pawns. White should always remember that the key element in this endgame is the natural superiority of his nimble knight. Will he?

33 Nd4?

Why use the great knight as a clumsy defender of an unimportant pawn? After the obvious 33 Nxg7 Bxf3 34 Ke1 White has a valuable passed f-pawn and fantastic winning chances.

33 . . .   g5!

Black on his part makes it so much more difficult for White to create a passed kingside pawn.

34 Ke1   h6!
35 Kd2?!

White makes it easy for Black to coordinate his bishop and pawns.

Again the nimble knight should be energized by 35 Nf5!.

35 . . .   Bg6
36 f4!

Because of White's dilly-dallying, there are no simple direct ways to make progress. The text move is quite correct, yet does carry some practical risks, in particular because White is in time trouble and the time control is not reached until move 40.

36 . . .   gxf4
37 Ne6   f3
38 Nd4??

White seems to have a fixation about never using his knight for attacking. Correct is the obvious 38 Nf4 Be4 39 Nxd3. It should be rather clear that after 39 . . . Bxd3? 40 Kxd3 the active king must give White the superior chances. In fact the endgame is won: 40 . . . Kc6 41 Ke3 Kc5 (Or 41 . . . Kd6 42 Kxf3 Ke5 43 Ke3 h5 44 f4+! Kf5 45 Kd4 and White's a-pawn will queen ahead of Black's h-pawn.) 42 Kxf3 Kd4 43 Kf4 Kd3 44 Ke5 d4 45 Kd5! h5 46 h4! Ke2 47 Kxd4 Kxf2 48 Kc5 and again the a-pawn will be the victor. Even though it is not obvious at the *moment* that White plays 39 Nxd3 that the king + pawn endgame is won, it should be certain that it is superior and that it carries no risk of losing. Therefore Black must avoid 39 . . . Bxd3? and continue with 39 . . . Kc6. The Argentine international master then recommends 40 Ke3! Kb5 41 Ne1! Kxa5 42 Nxf3. White has finally created a passed f-pawn, has complete control of the blockading d4 square and still the superior chances.

38 . . .   Be4

There is something grotesque about this position: White's play has consisted of going back and forth around the d4 square and giving up a pawn for nothing. Therefore, it is Black who now has the advantage.

39 Ke3   Kc7
40 Nxf3??

The final sin. White exchanges off his superior minor piece to enter an immediately losing K + P endgame. The knight had to be retained: 40 Ne6+ Kd6 41 Nd4 with fair drawing chances.

40 . . .   Bxf3
White resigns

After 41 Kxf3 d4! 42 h4 h5 White's king must move and allow the d-pawn to queen.

Even more enlightening is what happens from Diagram 45, which is from a simultaneous exhibition game V. Korchnoi – Smith & Kolkey, California 1977, after White's 23rd move. Jonathan Kolkey submitted it to me with the query "How on earth did we lose this endgame a pawn ahead?" Black lost it because he did not have a clue regarding the principles of playing rook + pawn endgames. On the other hand, the Grandmaster always knew what to do. And remember that Black had available much more thinking time than White.

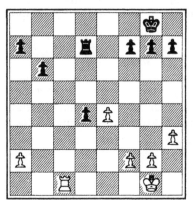

45

Since Black's troubles are so characteristic of other less experienced and less knowledgeable players, I am presenting a rather detailed blow-by-blow account.

The three key elements in the position are:

Black has a one pawn majority on the queenside; White has a similar one on the kingside. Since Black's king can presently stop White's extra king side pawn, whereas White's king cannot do the same to Black's extra queenside pawn, Black's majority is the more dangerous one. Moreover, in a K + P endgame, it is probably decisive. The kings are equivalently placed.

Both rooks are well placed: White's on an open file and Black's effectively behind the passed pawn.

Black's overriding advantage obviously comes from the extra pawn in the form of a passed d-pawn. However, it can neither be promoted, nor is it securely protected. The correct use of it is as a decoy, to tie up White's pieces long enough so that Black can do irreparable damage elsewhere.

The position is won for Black if he plays very resolutely at the start. Otherwise the win will evaporate. For White to have drawing prospects, his king must be able to effectively blockade the d-pawn by being on d3 and his rook must be activated. In the game White is able to achieve both of these goals (because of Black's irrelevant play) and he even managed to win! This is how it came to pass:

23 . . .   Kf8?!

The first misstep. The mate threat must be attended to, but why such a "modest" move? Indicated is 23 . . . f6! which allows . . . Kf7 *and* helps contain White's majority. Best play thereafter is 24 Kf1 d3! (Passed pawns must be pushed— here it immobilizes White's king.) 25 Rc8+ Kf7 26 Ke1 and now strongest and most thematic is further activation of Black's rook with 26 . . . Rd4! (H. Lyman). If White defends with 27 f3, Black wins easily by 27 . . . Ra4. Therefore, White's only try is the active 27 Rc7+ Kg6 28 Rxa7, but then 28 . . . Rxe4+ 29 Kd2 (29 Kf1?? d2) 29 . . . Re2+ 30 Kxd3 Rxf2 will annihilate White's kingside. For instance, 31 g4 Rf3+ 32 Kc4 Rxh3 33 Kb5 Rh4 34 Ra4 Kg5 35 Kxb6 f5! 36 Ra7 fxg4 37 Rxg7+ Kf4 and Black's two connected passed pawns will win easily enough against White's a-pawn.

24 Kf1   Ke7?

Correct is again 24 . . . d3! 25 Rc8+ Ke7 26 Ke1 Rd4!. Then 27 Rc7+ Ke6 28 Rxa7 Rxe4+ leads to an endgame equivalent to the one discussed in the previous note. The key is having the correct plan. Even though here Black is something like a tempo behind, what really matters is to play according to the logic of the position!

25 Ke2!   Kd6?

Black seems completely oblivious of the need to make some use of the d-pawn + rook behind the pawn combination. Still correct was to push the d-pawn: 25 . . . d3+ 26 Kd2 Ke6. This would give Black's rook some breathing room. Black is reluctant to push the d-pawn because he is afraid that it will become weak. Of course, it is just as weak on d4 and without generating any benefits!

26 Kd3!

White now has equality as Black's d-pawn is completely harmless. In R + P endgames, the proper blockader is the king and Korchnoi has rushed his king to the most active blockading square. In the meantime, note that Black has achieved nothing with his strength, i.e. the passed d-pawn even with the rook behind it.

26 . . .	Ke5
27 g3	g5
28 Rf1	h6?

Without a point, especially if Black exchanges next move. In that case, the text is even counterproductive, since on h6 the h-pawn is considerably weaker than on h7. If Black wanted to reinforce his g-pawn, then 28 . . . f6 is the logical way. The best, however, is 28 . . . Rc7!, activating the rook. The active rook is of utmost value in R + P endgames. Black plays the whole game essentially without his rook, whereas White's rook goes everywhere.

| 29 f4+ | gxf4 |

In point of fact this is no worse than 29 . . . Ke6, yet the lack of logic behind 28 . . . h6? is now apparent.

| 30 gxf4+ | Ke6 |
| 31 Rc1! | |

Black's king has been pushed back and the rook again grabs the most important open file, thereby not only activating itself but also keeping its counterpart docile.

31 . . .	f6
32 Rc6+	Rd6!
33 Rc7	

Exchanging rooks would be erroneous, because Black would be left with the advantage of the outside passed pawn in a K + P endgame.

33 . . .	Rd7
34 Rc6+	Rd6
35 Rc8!	

White has made so much progress from the start of this endgame that he now, understandably, wants more than a draw.

35 . . .   Kd7?

What can be the point of this move? It is the rook that needs activation, not the king! The king has already been running around as if without its head. As a broad comment on Black's play, it can be said that he loses because he is afraid to do anything against the Grandmaster. Black has done nothing with his d-pawn, nothing with his rook and now misses a chance to start using his queenside majority. Correct and necessary was 35 . . . b5! 36 Rh8 Ra6 37 Rxh6 Kf7! (after 37 . . . Rxa2?!, dangerous is 38 e5) with Black probably having equal chances in a unbalanced position.

36 Rh8   Kc6
37 Rxh6   Kc5
38 h4!

Passed pawns must be pushed— and Korchnoi demonstrates this at the very first chance that he has.

38 . . .   b5
39 Rh5+   Kc6?

And if Black wanted to play with the king, then mandatory was 39 . . . Kb4!?. Not that it's sufficient (White can play for example, 40 Rd5), but Black can hope to create some complications. Playing the text is like dying with one's boots on.

40 Rf5!   a6

Why not "risk" 40 . . . a5?

41 h5   Kd7
42 Rd5
Black resigns

The outside passed pawn— White's h-pawn—is the winner once more in a K + P endgame.

8

How to Win a Won Endgame

To gain a good result, it is imperative that the player wins his "won" games. The won game can be characterized either by a material or positional superiority. The material advantage of a pawn, where the weaker side has no compensation for its loss, should be sufficient for a win under normal conditions. Or alternatively the positional advantage could be so large, *that with correct play*, gain of material will result and thereby an ultimate victory. There is hardly a better way of learning in how to go about winning a won game than by watching how the top players in the country do it. The following examples are from the 1978 US Championship, which also doubled as the zonal tournament for the world championship cycle.

But first some general *principles*. To win a won game try to act in accordance with the following principles:

Establish and follow a clear plan.
Don't allow counterplay.

Avoid unclear or unnecessary complications.
Be careful.
Never be in a hurry, either with respect to time or number of moves. There is no extra prize for winning a game with lots of time left on the clock or for winning in fifty rather than sixty moves.
Hold on to material advantage.
When ahead in material, continually try to simplify the position by exchanging *pieces*.
Aim for the basic positions known as theoretical wins.

Let us now illustrate the above principles with actual examples, starting with those where already exists a material advantage, Diagram 46, A Soltis – B. Zuckerman after Black's 41st move, shows White a pawn up for which Black has no apparent compensation. The extra pawn is on the queenside in the form of a 3 P vs 1 P majority.

(see following diagram)

60

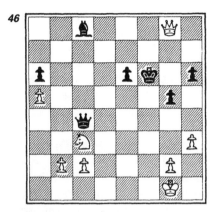

46

White's general winning procedure must consist of exploiting his queenside pawn majority, while at the same time preventing potential counterplay resulting from Black's Q + B + passed e-pawn combinations. Let's see how Soltis brings home the point with fine technique:

42 Qh7!

Not only preventing Black's . . . Bb7, but the attack on the h-pawn forces Black to deactivate his queen.

42 . . .	Qc5+
43 Kh1	Qf8

Of course, 43 . . . Qxa5? loses the bishop after 44 Qh8+.

44 b4!

Thanks to simple tactics (44 . . . Qxb4?? 45 Qh8+ and White wins

the bishop while protecting his knight) White gets his queenside going.

44 . . .	Ke5
45 Qe4+	Kd6
46 Qc4!	

After White's queen has forced Black's queen away from the center it gladly establishes itself there. Again 46 . . . Bb7?? is prevented: 47 Qc5+ wins the queen.

46 . . .	Ke5
47 b5!	

Continuing with the indicated plan of creating passed pawn(s) on the queenside.

47 . . .	axb5
48 Nxb5	

Notice how White has been achieving his objectives while keeping Black completely stymied. Black has no attractive move left, e.g. 48 . . . Ba6? 49 Qd4+ Kf5 50 Qf2+ and White wins one queen.

48 . . .	Qd8
49 Qc3+!	

Prior to exchanging queens, White chases Black's king further from the queenside. Black's reply is forced as 49 . . . Ke4? or 49 . . . Kf5? loses the bishop to 50 Qxc8!.

| 49 . . . | Kf4 |
| 50 Qc7+! | |

Unquestionably this is not the only way to win, but it is the clearest way. White simplifies the position by the exchange of queens, after which the a-pawn is a powerful queening threat.

50 . . .	Qxc7
51 Nxc7	Ke5
52 a6!	

Passed pawns must be pushed!

52 . . .	Kd6
53 a7	Bb7
54 a8=Q	

Transforming the material advantage of a pawn into the basic winning advantage of having the outside passed pawn in a K + P endgame.

54 . . .	Bxa8
55 Nxa8	Kc6
56 Kg1	Kb7
57 Kf2	Kxa8
58 Ke3!	

White aims for the basic position in this sort of endgame and goes for Black's passed pawn first. Even though White's outside passed pawn is only of minimum "outsidedness" (a b-pawn or a-pawn

would give an easier win), it is sufficient to win.

58 . . .	Kb7
59 Kd4	Kc6
60 Ke5	Kd7
61 g4!	

White handles the position in the clearest possible way. The g-pawn is safe from an attack by Black's king and White will utilize his c-pawn to deflect Black's king from the e-pawn. There is less logic in 61 Kf6, though it also wins if White plays after 61 . . . Kd6, 62 c4!.

61 . . .	Ke7
62 c4	Kd7
63 c5	Kc6
64 Kxe6	Kxc5
65 Kf6	

The graphic reason why the outside passed pawn usually wins in K + P endgames: after the passed pawns disappear, the "inside" king is closer to the remaining pawns.

65 . . .	Kd5
66 Kg6	Ke4
67 Kxh6	Kf4
68 Kh5	Kg3
69 Kxg5	Kxh3
70 Kh5	
Black resigns	

Appearing considerably more complicated is the starting position from Diagram 47, E. Mednis – B. Zuckerman, after Black's 21st move. However, it can be broken down into some basics readily enough. At the moment White is a piece up for a pawn, but has fallen behind in development as a direct result of having won the piece. Black will also win White's f-pawn and thus have two pawns for the piece, which is still insufficient compensation. White's first order of business is to complete the development of his queenside; then make sure that Black's passed f-pawn is no threat and finally to utilize the extra piece for winning purposes. The time situation on the clock is also worth mentioning. Up to now I had used only 50 minutes and thus had still 1 hour and 40 minutes to reach the time control on move 40. Throughout the coming play I made sure that I fully utilized my remaining time. I felt sure that with correct

play White's position must be won. Therefore why rush and give the opponent any chances?

22 Nc3!

The only move worth considering: the knight move prevents . . . e2, controls the key e4 square and connects the rooks. Obviously 22 fxe3?? loses to 22 . . . Bxe3+.

22 . . .   exf2+

Being a piece down, Black wants to keep the position as complicated as possible. Therefore wrong is 22 . . . Rxf2? 23 Rxf2! exf2+ 24 Kf1 and White will quickly consolidate and capture the f-pawn.

23 Kh1	Rf5
24 Bg3	Raf8
25 Rad1!	

With the queen's knight out, the next step is to develop the queen's rook. But where? I considered 25 Racl, with the plan of exerting pressure on Black's c-pawn. Yet that hardly seemed like the most important strategic plan. The rook on d1 controls a useful open file and makes it therefore much harder for Black to come up with any counterplay.

25 . . .   h5
26 h3!

After the game my opponent asked why I didn't play the active 26 h4. To me that seemed to lead to some weakening of the kingside and I didn't see any need to do so.

26 . . .	h4
27 Bh2	Kg7
28 g4!	

In order to minimize potential counterplay, White clears the g2 square for his king, thereby preventing any back rank mates and allowing the king to participate in stopping the f-pawn. The only slight disadvantage of the move is that f3 now is accessible to Black's rooks. Black can't afford to exchange pawns: 28 . . . hxg3 e.p.?! 29 Bxg3 followed by 30 Kg2 and the f-pawn's days are numbered.

28 . . .	Rf3
29 Kg2	Kg6
30 Rd7	R8f7

While Black has no constructive continuation (30 . . . Re3 is parried by 31 Nd1), the voluntary exchange of a pair of rooks is completely prospectless.

| 31 Rxf7 | Rxf7 |
| 32 Be5! | |

A multipurpose move: the bishop in general stands better on e5 than h2, the advance of the e-pawn is prevented, the d4 square is guarded, and the b-pawn is protected. White maximizes his prospects and minimizes Black's chances.

32 . . .	c6
33 Ne4	Rd7
34 Nxf2	

An obvious consequence of Black's 30th. Black has lost his only pride and is close to the end.

| 34 . . . | Rd2 |
| 35 Kf3 | |

Getting out of the pin so that the extra piece can be used for offense.

35 . . .	Rc2
36 Bc3	Kh6
37 Ne4!	

White's pieces are in a bit of a bind and to activate them White sacrifices the h-pawn. Yet this was not done on any general principle, but based on a concrete calculation. I still had over 30 minutes of time left and thus could calculate the coming "complications" to their mathematical end. A safe general move was 37 Be5 (thereby establishing the same position as after Black's 35th move), followed by 38 Ne4.

37 . . .	Rh2
38 Be5!	Rxh3+
39 Kg2	Re3
40 Rf6+	Kg7

leads to an elementary finish. My main line calculation was: 40 . . . Kh7 41 Nxg5+ Kg8 42 Rg6+ Kf8 43 Bd6+ Ke8 44 Rxe6+ Rxe6 45 Nxe6 Kd7 46 Bc5!. Though this could be considered to involve looking ten moves ahead at move 37, the position is simple enough to allow a master to do it quite easily—that is if he takes the time to do so!

41 Rf3+1

But with the coming endgame available, there is no need to look for "complications" at this stage.

41 . . .	Kg6
42 Rxe3	Bxe3
43 Bc7	

Black resigns

After winning Black's a-pawn, White will have a passed a-pawn to go with the extra piece. For this endgame starting with move 22, I used 1 hour and 25 minutes. Considering the relative simplicity of the position, this can be considered to be a lot. But why not? Remember that no special prize is awarded for playing a won position quickly. It's only the end result that counts!

And now for an endgame with material equality but which must be considered won because of positional considerations. Diagram 48, L. Kavalek – A. Soltis, after Black's 30th move, shows a position "won" for White, for these reasons: (1) White has control of both open files, (2) White's bishop is more active than Black's, (3) White's knight will soon be much more active than Black's, (4) White has the superior pawn formation. In particular, Black's a-pawn is weak and if Black tries to protect it via . . . b6, then the b-pawn will have become weak. It is quite instructive how Kavalek converts the above advantages into a win. As Black puts up tough resistance, White's task is not easy at all. Even though the commentator can confidently tag positions such as this one as "wins", it must be stressed that in real life they do not *win themselves*,

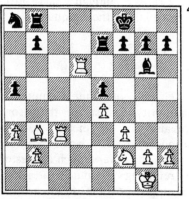

48

but require a considerable amount of thinking and care. Simple perhaps with hindsight, yet note how Kavalek does it with foresight:

31 Ng4   f6
32 Ne3

White's knight is excellently placed in the center and if necessary is ready to head for c4, d5, or f5.

32 . . .   Nc7
33 Rb6

Black's last move not only prevented White's Nd5, but also carried the . . . Nb5 threat. White therefore prevents the activation of Black's knight.

33 . . .   Be8

bringing the bishop back for defense of the queenside and reactivation of the . . . Nb5 "threat". Necessarily, though this gives White's knight the f5 square.

34 Nf5   Na8
35 Rd6!

The bulk of White's immediate superiority consists of the strong pressure that his pieces exert on various parts of Black's position. Thus White is very much interested in retaining as much attacking power as possible until he has

achieved some more tangible advantages. Instead 35 Nxe7?! Nxb6 would have lightened Black's defensive task. Now 35 . . . Rd7 is not satisfactory as after 36 Bd5! Rxd6 37 Nxd6 Black's b-pawn is under severe pressure while White's three remaining pieces control the board completely. Black therefore attempts to exchange a pair of rooks under more favorable circumstances.

35 . . .   Rc7
36 Rcd3!

As already mentioned in the previous note, the first phase of White's plan consists of utilizing his attacking prospects to either gain material or a permanent positional superiority. Therefore, he eschews any routine exchange of pieces. Despite a first superficial appearance, the text move does not allow Black counterplay because the coming single rook incursion is completely toothless.

36 . . .   Rc1+
37 Kf2   Rb1
38 Rd2   Nc7
39 Ba2   Ra1

This turns out to be a loss of time and thus the immediate 39 . . . Rc1! was better—not that this has a major bearing on the course of the game.

40 Bd5!

Tempting Black to play 40 . . . Nxd5?! as after 41 exd5! White would have a very strong passed pawn—a clear tangible achievement.

| 40 . . . | Rc1 |
| 41 Rb6 | Bc6 |

Forced, as the b-pawn is threatened and 41 . . . Nxd5?! is again inferior because of 42 exd5!.

42 Bxc6!

White is agreeable to this exchange, because he sees that he will either have excellent chances to win the b-pawn and/or strong play along the d-file, including control of d7. Starting with Diagram 48, the play has advanced sufficiently so that tangible benefits can come from exchanges.

| 42 . . . | Rxc6 |
| 43 Rd6! | |

This is the move to both keep the pressure and prevent meaningful counterplay. Instead after 43 Rxc6?! bxc6 Black's rook would have good prospects along the b-file. However, if now 43 . . . Rxb6 44 Rxb6 Na8 45 Rd6 Rc8 46 Ke3! and White's remaining pieces control the board. Thus Black

decides to try for at least some cosmetic activity with the text move.

43 . . .	Rc2+
44 Kg3	Na8
45 Rb3	a4

Andy and I were rooming together and the position after White's 45th move appeared during his adjournment analysis. The question became: how should Black continue? On general principles it seemed to me that 45 . . . b5!? is the best that Black has. However, I soon went to bed and Andy decided that since my suggestion isn't fully satisfactory either, that he prefers the text. However, in his late night analysis he had overlooked White's coming 50th move.

| **46 Rbd3!** | Nc7 |

The poor placement of the knight makes 46 . . . Rxb2?? impossible (47 Rd8+ wins the knight).

47 Rd8+!

White is well justified in exchanging one of his active rooks for Black's defensive one, as this leads to the forced win of a pawn. Note how the incessant pressure on Black's position has led to material gain for White.

| 47 . . . | Rxd8 |
| 48 Rxd8+ | Kf7 |

If 48 . . . Ne8, 49 Rb8! and the threat of 50 Nd6 forces the win of the b-pawn.

| 49 Rd7+ | Kf8 |
| 50 Nxg7! | |

Black would get counterplay after 50 Rxg7? Ne6! followed by 51 . . . Nf4. However, after the text, Black's knight doesn't have access to e6, while White himself threatens 51 Rxc7! Rxc7 52 Ne6+. Since 50 . . . Kg8 is quite hopeless after 51 Nh5 etc, Black tries a knight tour.

50 . . .	Nb5
51 Ne6+	Ke8
52 Rxb7	

White's positional superiority had led to a two-pawn advantage. During the next few moves White ensures that he keeps this material advantage, while giving Black no counterplay. Since 52 . . . Rxb2?? loses to either 53 Rxb5 or 53 Nc7+, Black's knight must move again.

52 . . .	Nd6
53 Ra7!	Rxb2
54 Rxa4	Kf7
55 Nc5	Ra2
56 Ra7+	Kg6
57 Ne6	
Black resigns	

He is two pawns down and faced with the threat of 58 Nf8+. Further resistance would be truly pointless.

9

Winning Rook + Minor Piece Endgames

The numerical value of a minor piece—bishop or knight—is about three pawns. Therefore, from a strictly numerical standpoint, the bishop and knight are equivalent. But which is the more valuable in an endgame? Well, it depends on the particular endgame. Most readers no doubt know that the bishop is more effective in open positions where there is play on both sides of the board, whereas the knight is better suited for infighting in a blocked position.

What happens when a major piece—queen or rook—is added to the minor piece? It matters very much *which* major piece is added. The queen + knight combination is more effective in general than queen + bishop. The reason is that the queen already has all the long-range power that is required and the knight adds valuable flexibility to it. However, rook + bishop is generally more effective than rook + knight. Even though the rook, of

course, has no diagonal capability, in combination with the bishop this team has extremely strong long-range power.

The bishop is characteristically the superior minor piece in positions of the type of Diagram 49, K. Rogoff – W. Lombardy, 1978 US Championship, after Black's 24th move. Material is even, Black has no chronic weaknesses and Black even has the queenside pawn majority. Yet, nevertheless, it is

49

White who has a significant advantage. How come? Well, a deeper consideration shows the following actual situation: (1) White's kingside pawn majority has led to significant central control (e-pawn!), whereas Black's queenside majority is lame, (2) in the existing open type of position, the bishop is superior to the knight, (3) specifically, White's bishop is powerfully placed, exerting extremely strong pressure against Black's knight + a-pawn configuration, (4) White has imminent control of the only open file while Black's king's rook is awkwardly placed. The net result is that White's position is close to being won and in the following few moves Rogoff delivers a perfect example of "how to win an almost won position":

| 25 a4! | h6 |
| 26 Bc5! | |

White's progress is clear: with his 25th move he ensured further pressure against Black's queenside and his last move gives him the d-file. With his reply, Black hopes to oppose rooks there, but thanks to time gained by attack on the knight, White is able to double rooks for complete mastery of the file.

| 26 ... | Ree8 |
| 27 a5 | Nc4 |

28 Rd4	Ne5
29 Rad1	g5
30 Kf2!	

Excellent strategic *and practical* play. Through his 29th move, White has raced to establish complete control over the position. Yet now it is not so clear what can be achieved next. Therefore White takes "time out" from active operations to centralize the king for potential future benefit. He also puts the following question to Black: "What can you do to improve your position?"

| 30 ... | h5? |

There is a tendency, in master and amateur circles alike, to push pawns when short of time and short of an attractive plan. So here too, but the damage is to the pusher, who now has weak h- and g-pawns. According to Rogoff, he saw no forced win if Black had played 30 . . . Reb8! with the idea of the liberating 31 . . . b6.

| 31 Rd6! | Nc4 |

chasing the rook to where it wants to go. However, by now there are no satisfactory moves, e.g. 31 . . . Kg7 allows the nasty pin 32 Bd4, whereas 31 . . . Kh7 is met by 32 Rf6.

| 32 Rh6 | Kg7 |

Equally unsatisfactory is 32 . . h4 33 a6! b6 (33 . . . bxa6 34 Rxc6 a5 35 Bd4 Rec8 36 Rh6!) 34 Bd4 Ne5 35 Bxe5 Rxe5 36 Rxc6.

| 33 Rxh5 | Kg6 |
| 34 g4 | Rac8?! |

Of course, Black has less than no compensation for the missing pawn. Even so, the follow-up via the text move seems to make no chess sense That's because it *makes no chess sense* and in fact was a "forced move". Short of time, Black had picked up the queen's rook and placed it on d8 (without releasing his hand) to play the reasonably thematic 34 . . . Rad8. Yet immediately he had noted the refutation: 35 Rxd8 Rxd8 36 Rxg5+! Kxg5 37 Be7+. Thus of moves with the queen's rook, the text is the best there was. Of the unforced moves, Black's best try was 34 . . . b6.

35 Rd4!	Ne5
36 Bxa7	Rcd8
37 Ke2!	

Note how useful White's 30th move has become for denying Black any counterplay.

37 . . .	f6
38 h4	Nf7
39 hxg5	Rxd4
40 Bxd4	f5!?

An ingenious try to complicate matters in time pressure. Unfortunately for Black, the time control has been reached for White and he had plenty of time to consider the position and seal the killing . . .

41 Rh4!
Black resigns

Black resigned without continuing the game as he will be three pawns down in a hopeless position: 41 . . . Kxg5 42 Rh5+ followed by 43 Rxf5; 41 . . . Nxg5 42 gxf5+; 41 . . . fxg4 42 Rxg4; 41 . . . fxe4 42 f4! followed by 43 Bf6 and 44 f5+.

The times when R + N are better than R + B are usually associated with situations where the knight is significantly superior to the bishop. An extreme case is shown in Diagram 50, E. Mednis – R. Byrne, New Jersey 1959, after White's 36th

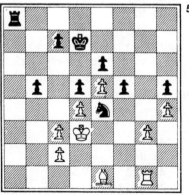

50

move. With just minor pieces on the board, White would have drawing chances, since the blocked position makes penetration by Black's king difficult. However, the additional attacking power of Black's rook easily overwhelms White's position:

| 36 . . . | Ra1! |
| 37 Rf1 | |

Already White must acquiesce to loss of material as a king move allows 37 . . . Nxc3 and a rook move 37 . . . Nxg3. However, since White cannot safeguard his position, Black first prevents any white counterplay along the g-file.

37 . . .	Ke8
38 Rg1	Kf7
39 Rf1	c6
40 Rg1	Rc1
41 Ke2	Rxc2+
42 Kd1	Ra2
43 Rf1	Ke8
44 Rf3	Kd7

Earlier on Black had a choice of which pawn to win. He chose c2 so as to penetrate on the queenside and still leave g3 as a chronic weakness.

45 Re3	c5!
46 dxc5	Nxc5
47 Re2	Ra4
48 Rb2?	

A blunder in a lost position. 48 Re3 would have prolonged matters.

48 . . .	Ra1+
49 Kd2	Rxe1!
50 Rxb5	Kc6
51 Rb8	Rxe5
52 Rh8	Re4
53 Rxh5	Rg4
54 Rh8	Rxg3
55 h5	Kd6
56 h6	Ke5
57 Ke2	Ne4
White resigns	

However, there is another type of position where the knight is better, even though based on a routine evaluation the bishop side should be superior. This is a rather open position with pawns on both sides, but where the pawn structure is such that the bishop can not do any damage but where the knight has real prospects. This situation is exemplified by Diagram 51, J.

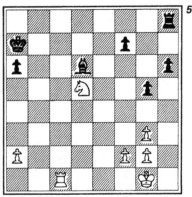
51

Smejkal – P. Nikolic, Novi Sad 1982, after Black's 31st move. Nothing in White's position is vulnerable to Black's bishop. On the other hand, White's knight can make excellent use of the hole on f5 to attack the h6 pawn in particular and the whole kingside pawn phalanx in general. It is White, therefore, who has the superior chances in a riskless position. But please note that if Black's g-pawn would be back on g6, then the chances would be quite equal. In our position, however, Black's defensive task is quite unpleasant and he lost as follows:

32 Kf1!

At the moment White's rook and knight stand well enough so that White gets ready to activate the king.

32 ...   Re8?!

Trying to prevent the king from reaching the e-file seems logical, but in the long run cannot be accomplished. A better defensive method would be 32 ... Rd8! 33 Ne3 Kb7 34 Nf5 Bf8 35 Ke2 Rd5! with White just slightly better. Even though Black would like to improve his kingside pawn safety, 32 ... h5? is too weakening: 33 Rc6 Be5 34 Nb4 a5 35 Nd3 and White wins material.

33 Rc6	**Re6**

Here too 33 ... Rd8! is better (34 Ne3 Kb7).

34 g4	**Be5**
35 Rc2	**Kb7**
36 Ke2!	**Rd6**
37 Ne3	**Rf6**
38 Nc4	**Rf4?**

Black's pieces will now be forced into a clumsy defensive regrouping. After 38 ... Bd4 39 f3 Bc5 (Minev) Black's position would remain fully defensible.

39 g3!	**Rd4**

Of course 39 ... Rxg4? loses to 40 Kf3, After 39 ... Re4+ 40 Kf3 Re1 41 Re2! Rxe2 42 Kxe2 Bc7 43 Kd3 White has a significantly superior minor piece endgame because of the more active king and Black's chronically weak kingside. Therefore, leaving the rooks on is logical, but does not affect White's inherent superiority.

40 Ne3	**Rd8**
41 Nf5	**Rh8**
42 Kf3	**f6**

The problems on Black's kingside are now obvious. The immediate 42 ... h5? 43 gxh5 Rxh5 44 Kg4 drops a pawn.

43	Ke4!	h5
44	gxh5	Rxh5
45	Ne3!	Rh1
46	Kf5	

A position just about as para-doxical as our starting one: Black's rook and bishop *look* active, but it is White who is about to win mate-rial!

46	. . .	Rb1
47	Nd5	Rf1
48	f4	gxf4
49	gxf4	Ba1
50	Rc7+!	Kb8
51	Rc4!	Rb1
52	a4!	Kb7
53	Nxf6	Rd1
54	Ng4	Kb6
55	Ne5	Rd4
56	Ke6	Rd1
57	Re4!	Bc3
58	f5	

Black resigns

His "active" R + B cannot do anything, whereas White's f-pawn will continue on its merry march.

Of course, each side can have the same minor pieces and the position can still be significantly favorable to one side. An instructive example is Diagram 52, J. Tarjan – L. Christ-iansen, 1978 US Championship, af-ter Black's 25th move. A cool eva-luation must show that White is considerably better. He has a useful passed a-pawn and the overall more

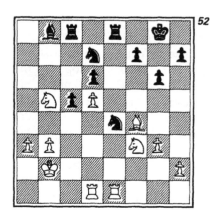

active position. In particular, Black's d-pawn is a very serious weakness and Black's bishop is rele-gated to being a third class citizen in having to protect the pawn from a very passive location. Black has nothing to counter these problems as his kingside majority can't be readily mobilized and Black's pieces are too passive to try to bother White's somewhat loose king location. White's first step is to put more pressure on the d-pawn by trying to exchange off a defender:

    26 Ng5!   **Nxg5?!**

falling in too easily with White's plans. More thematic was to rein-force the knight outpost with 26 . . . Ndf6!.

    27 Bxg5   Ne5
    28 Kc3!

The threat of 28 . . . Nd3+ does force a king move and White prefers c3 so that Black's rook does not get to e2 with check in variations such as 28 Kc2 Nf3 29 Rxe8+ Rxe8 30 Bf4 Re2+. But now after 28 . . . Bc7 White would play 29 Kc2!, as the fact that Black's bishop would then be en prise makes the above line fruitless for Black.

28 . . .	f5?!

fundamentally weakening the knight's status on e5. A better defensive set-up was 28 . . . Kg7 followed by 29 . . . f6.

29	Bf4	Kf7
30	a4!	

Passed pawns must be pushed!

30	. . .	Bc7
31	Kc2!	Kf6
32	h4	Kf7

There is no way Black can deploy his forces to cover all his weak spots. This allows White's a-pawn to move forward decisively.

33	a5!	Red8
34	a6	Nf3
35	Re6	Rd7
36	Kb2!	

One more sophisticated king maneuver: White makes sure that Black never gets in . . . Nd4 *with check.*

36	. . .	Ra8
37	Nxc7	

Time to harvest.

37	. . .	Rxc7
38	Bxd6	Rcc8

Or 38 . . . Rca7 39 Bxc5 Rxa6 40 Rxa6! Rxa6 41 d6! and the d-pawn will cost Black his knight.

39	Re7+	Kf6
40	Re6+	Kf7
41	Re7+	Kf6
42	a7	Nd4
43	Rb7	

Black resigns

There is no satisfactory way to cope with threats such as 44 Bxc5 or 44 Re1; 43 . . . Nf3 is answered by 44 Rd3 etc.

10

The Value of the Passed Rook Pawn in Knight Endgames

How useful is a passed rook pawn for direct queening purposes? Well, it depends—BUT it is usually the worst passed pawn to have. In K + P endgames the defending king can often save itself by a stalemate. The rook pawn is also the inferior passed pawn in queen, rook and often in bishop endgames. All these are long-range pieces, and thus have no difficulty with stopping any kind of a passed pawn from far away. Moreover, because there is only one side to a rook pawn, the king has it easier in stopping it, since it only has to worry about attacks from one side of the board, rather than both sides, as with other pawns. Furthermore, the attacking king can penetrate only from one side and often has insufficient scope when in front of the pawn.

However, in knight endgames just the converse is true: the rook pawn is the strongest passed pawn. There are two reasons for this. Firstly, since the knight is a short-range piece, it has great difficulty in stopping far away passed pawns and the rook pawn is always the most outside passed pawn. Secondly, once the rook pawn has reached the 7th rank, the knight by itself cannot cope with the enemy king and thus will be lost.

How to utilize a passed rook pawn to win superior endgames and draw inferior ones will be shown from the following examples.

The first step in utilizing a passed rook pawn is to obtain or "create" it. Some basic but nice tactics do the job from Diagram 53, G. Bonner – A. Medina, Haifa Olympiad 1976,

(see following diagram)

Black to move. At first glance it seems that White should have no trouble, since White's doubled b-pawns can stop the Black a- and b-pawn duo. Yet Black is able to exploit White's lack of an a-pawn with the electrifying:

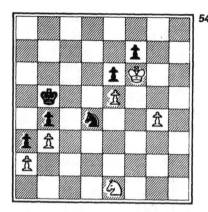

| 1 ... | Nc3!! |
| 2 bxc3 | |

White's attacked knight has no moves and can't be defended. Of course 2 Nxc3 dxc3 will give Black an unstoppable a-pawn for nothing.

| 2 ... | a4! |

Now Black has a passed rook pawn and the knight cannot cope with it.

3 cxd4	cxd4!
4 c3	a3
White resigns	

More straightforward tactics allow Black to save Diagram 54, H. J. Hecht – A. Pomar, Olot 1971, Black to move. White's winning plan is clear: after capturing the f-pawn, he will queen his g-pawn.

Black's only prospects rest with getting into White's queenside, though no simple means are apparent. Black played:

| 1 ... | Kc5 |
| 2 Kxf7 | |

White has nothing better than executing *his* plan. Attempts at passive defense boomerang: 2 Nd3+ Kb5 3 Nc1?! Nf3 4 g5 Kc5! 5 Kxf7? (Correct is 5 Nd3+) 5 ... Nxg5+ 6 Kf6 Nf3 7 Kxe6 Kd4! 8 Ne2+ Ke3 9 Ng3 Kd3 10 Kd6 Nxe5! 11 Kxe5 Kc3 and at best White will draw.

| 2 ... | Nxb3!! |
| 3 axb3 | Kd4! |

Black has sacrificed the knight to get a passed a-pawn and White's knight is impotent in stopping it.

4 g5	Kc3!
5 g6	a2
6 g7	a1=Q
7 g8=Q	Qxe1
8 Qc8+	Kxb3
9 Qxe6+	

This Q + P endgame is drawn.

9 . . .	Kb2
10 Qf6	b3
11 e6+	Kc2
12 Qf5+	Kc1
13 e7	b2
14 Qc5+	Kd1
15 Qd4+	Kc2
16 Qc4+	Kd1!
17 Qd3+	Kc1
Draw	

Consider now Diagram 55, Cook – L. Portisch, Adelaide 1971, with White to move. Despite the reduced material, Black has some real winning chances since White's knight is misplaced and Black has

the more active position. Yet White could have drawn if he had realized the power of a passed a-pawn. Play continued:

1 Nh5	Ne4!
2 bxc4!	

It is in the interest of the defending side to exchange pawns *and* the c-pawn must be paid attention to. In the game White played 2 Ng7+ ?? and after 2 . . . Kf6 3 Ne8+ Kf7! he resigned, since if 4 Nc7, 4 . . . c3 and the c-pawn queens.

2 . . .	bxc4
3 Ke3	Kf7!
4 a4!	

Passed pawns must be pushed! Since White's trapped knight must be lost, the only chances rest with the a-pawn.

4 . . .	Kg6
5 Ng3!!	Nxg3
6 Kd4!	

It is imperative to eliminate the c-pawn. Therefore, wrong is 6 a5? Ne4 7 a6 c3, since 8 Kd3 fails to 8 . . . Nc5+ and 9 . . . Nxa6.

6 . . .	Ne2+
7 Kxc4	Nxf4
8 a5	Ne6
9 a6	Nc7
10 a7	f4

As shown by Yugoslav international master Maric, bringing back the king also doesn't win: 10 . . . Kf6 11 Kc5 Ke7 12 Kc6 Kd8 13 a8=Q+!! Nxa8 14 Kd5 and White both catches and captures Black's remaining pawn.

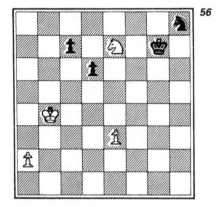

11 Kc5	f3
12 Kc6	Na8
13 Kb7	

We have now the single most important position in the knight vs. rook pawn endgame. The knight can not stand its ground and is captured. Our queen vs. pawn position is a standard book draw, since Black's king is too far away.

13 . . .	f2
14 Kxa8	f1=Q
15 Kb8	Qb5+
16 Ka8!	
Drawn	

Since, as we have seen in the previous two examples, the rook pawn can help draw inferior positions, it can be expected that it will lead to victories in superior positions. An excellent demonstration of this is Diagram 56, L. Pachman – A. Lombard, Mannheim 1975, after White's 46th move. White's passed a-pawn coupled with the momentary out-of-the-game location for Black's knight, does give White realistic

winning chances—despite the very meager amount of material remaining and the healthy condition of Black's pawns. Black now played:

46 . . .	Kf8?

After this careless move, Black is lost. He wants to keep free f7 for the return of his knight, but the immediate need was to prevent White's 48th move. Necessary is 46 . . . Kf7! and Black can draw if he continues to defend perfectly.

47 Nd5!	c6

Obviously 47 . . . c5+? allows White's king to march in after 48 Kb5.

48 Nf6!!	

The knight has a colossal and safe location here.

48 . . .	Ke7
49 a4!	Kd8

The knight cannot be captured: 49 . . . Kxf6? 50 a5 Ng6 51 a6 Ne7 52 a7 Nd5+ 53 Ka5 Nc7 54 Kb6 Na8+ 55 Kb7 and again the king + rook pawn on the 7th win against the knight.

50 a5	Nf7

50 . . . Kc7 fails to 51 Ne8+: (a) 51 . . . Kd7 52 a6! and (b) 51 . . . Kb7 52 Nxd6+.

51 a6	Kc8
52 Nd7!!	

covering the b8 square while being inviolate itself. We can now appreciate the value of having the knight establish itself on f6 on move 48.

52 . . .	Nd8
53 Ka5	Ne6
54 Nf6!	d5

Again 54 . . . Kc7 loses to 55 Ne8+, whereas 54 . . . Nc7 allows the simple 55 Kb6. Therefore, Black tries to mobilize his pawns.

55 Kb6	Nc7
56 a7	c5
57 Ne8!	Na8+
58 Kc6!	c4

Pushing the other pawn is no better: 58 . . . d4 59 Nd6+ Kd8 and now not 60 Kb7? because of 60 . . . dxe3 61 Kxa8 Kc7!! with a draw, but the simple 60 e4! d3 61 Nc4. Black's connected passed pawns are stopped and there is no way that he can cope with White's widely separated passed pawns.

59 Nd6+	Kd8
60 Nb5	
Black resigns	

After 60 . . . Kc8 White's simplest win is 61 Nc3! Nc7 62 Nxd5!.

By now it should be clear that if there is a passed rook pawn on the board, that side wants to simplify down if possible to a knight endgame. Conversely, the other side should strive to prevent this from happening. The kind of practical considerations that should come into play are shown from Diagram 57,

(see following diagram)

A Karpov – A Adorjan, Budapest 1973, after Black's 37th move. The position, though both unbalanced and complicated, can be broken down into various components for easier evaluation. White is up a pawn, but one of his h-pawns is *en prise*. The c-pawn, though passed and advanced, is well blockaded and vulnerable. Black has a passed

57

f-pawn and a strong and active bishop pair. It is Black who has the significantly more active position and therefore also the superior chances. Yet note now how quickly all this changes. Karpov keeps the strategic requirements in mind, whereas his opponent does not:

38 Nxa5

The passed a-pawn makes its appearance.

38 . . .   Bxa5??

Being in time pressure, Black sees that he can capture White's c-pawn and satisfies himself with that. But there was no reason at all to remove the bind that Black has over the position. After the correct 38 . . . f5! Black would retain his edge.

39 Rxa5	Nxc6?

overlooking the reply. Keeping the rooks on gave better chances for the draw. Therefore, correct is 39 . . . Bxc6.

40 Ra8!

With the rooks off, the power of the a-pawn increases dramatically.

40 . . .	Rxa8
41 Bxa8	Ne5?

True that the knight is in an unpleasant pin, but allowing a pure knight endgame is strategic suicide. 41 . . . Kf8 had to be tried.

42 Bxf3	Nxf3
43 a4!	Ne5

The knight has to head back. Black sealed this move and later resigned without resuming play. The logical continuation would be:

44 a5	Kf8
45 a6	Nc6
46 Kc4	Ke7
47 Kc5	Kd7
48 Nd5	Na7
49 Nf4!	

blockading Black's passed pawn and enabling White's next move.

49 . . .	Kc7
50 h5!	gxh5
51 Nxh5	f5
52 Nf4	

White wins

With the a-pawn tieing Black down on the queenside, the formerly puny doubled h-pawn will now advance decisively.

Part III

Drawing Inferior Endgames

Just like death and taxes, it is inevitable that every player will find himself in inferior positions. Since it happens to world champions, it will surely happen to the rest of us. And it is equally certain that part of the time the inferior middlegame will turn into an inferior endgame. Often this comes about "naturally": your opponent gains an advantage in the opening, keeps it throughout the middlegame and voluntarily prefers to enter a superior endgame. Or consider the following situation: your king is under such an attack that you are extremely happy to escape into an inferior endgame. Both of these important routes will be explored at some length later in the book.

No matter how it comes about, the important fact is that you find yourself in an unpleasant endgame. What to do? The first and single most important thing is to grit your teeth and say to yourself: "I have just begun to fight!" Such a fighting attitude is invaluable and is the major reason why great fighters like Reshevsky and Botvinnik have saved so many "lost" endgames.

Of course, you will also need the appropriate tools. The general principles covering both what not to do and what to do are discussed in Chapters 11, 12 and 13. The best known specific technique is to exchange off as many of the enemy pawns as possible and then sacrifice a minor piece for the last pawn(s). Then even though you are a piece down, you are safe because your opponent does not have sufficient mating material. Of course, achieving perpetual check or a threefold repetition of the position is just as useful in an endgame as a middlegame. There also are several specific technical endgames you want to aim for: 2 knights vs nothing, B + wrong colour rook pawn, R + B vs R, R + N vs R.

However, the specific area that I want to take a deeper look at is something that much too often is overlooked: achieving stalemate.

Obviously this is purely an endgame strategy. Stalemates are possible—and should be looked for—in all kinds of endgames. Yet the most important and common instances occur with maximum firepower (queen endgames) and minimum power (king endgames). These are thoroughly explored in Chapters 14 and 15.

11

What Not to Do in Inferior Endgames

Inferior endgames are tough to handle. Often just a relatively small inaccuracy is all that is required for the game to be unalterably lost. Therefore, it is absolutely mandatory *not* to make your difficult situation any worse. The four leading types of errors are discussed in this chapter—in the hope that you will always be on the lookout for them and therefore won't commit them:

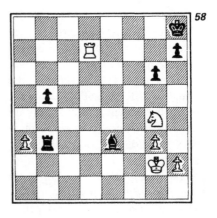

58

No. 1. If you neglect a threat, you will lose

Inferior positions are much more vulnerable to threats by the opponent than are superior ones. The threats are more numerous and the ultimate danger is greater. Therefore, be very careful regarding all potential threats. An extreme case is illustrated from Diagram 58, V. Hort – V. Antoshin, Budapest 1973, after White's 33rd move. Because Black's king is in the corner,

White has a very definite threat. However, Black was in considerable time pressure and played:

33 . . .   Bc1??

Protecting against a non-existent threat (34 Nxe3) and ignoring the real one. It may be somewhat risky to play 33 . . . Bg5 because of 34 h4 h5 35 Ne5, but fully satisfactory is 33 . . . Kg8!. Then after 34 Nf6+ Kf8 35 Nxh7+ Ke8, because of the threat to the a-pawn, White seems to have nothing better than to take perpetual check with 36 Nf6+ etc.

34 Nf6   Rb2+
35 Kh3
Black resigns

No. 2. If you allow unnecessary simplification, you will lose

When down material (i.e. pawn(s)) the rule of thumb is very clear: *Exchange pawns; do not exchange pieces.* (Conversely, the stronger side should exchange pieces, not pawns). You simply do not want to wind up in a routinely lost K+P endgame, or other simplified endgames where the lack of pieces means that you have no counterplay. A typical situation is shown in Diagram 59, H. J. Hecht – B. Spassky, Dortmund 1973, after

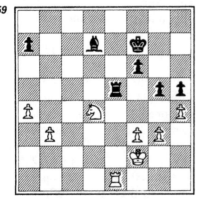

59

White's 50th move. White is a sound queenside pawn up and Black obviously has no compensation for this. Still, it is much too early to resign. Therefore, the question becomes: what is Black's best *practical* course?

50 . . .   Rxe1??

Surely, not this one! Why did Black think the resulting pawn-down minor piece endgame offered drawing chances? To hope to cope with White's queenside pawns Black will obviously need the services of an active rook. A reasonable defensive move therefore is 50 . . . Rc5.

51 Kxe1	**Ke7**
52 Kd2	**Kd6**
53 Kd3	**Ke5**
54 a5	**a6**
55 b4	

White prepares to create a passed pawn with a properly timed b5 break, and there will be nothing that Black can do about it. The attempt to get immediate counter-play by 55 . . . gxh4 (56 gxh4 Kf4) is foiled by the "zwischen-check" 56 f4+!: 56 . . . Kd5 57 gxh4 Bh3 58 Nb3 Bf1+ 59 Ke3 Bb5 60 Nd2 f5 61 Nf3 Kc4 62 Nd4! Kxb4 63 Nxf5 Kxa5 64 Nd6! and White will win on the kingside (analysis by Hecht). Nevertheless, this variation offers

Black more hope than the game
continuation.

55 ...	Kd5?!
56 Kc3!	gxh4
57 gxh4	Ke5
58 Kc4!	Kd6

Because b5 cannot be prevented,
Black is quite lost. If 58 . . . Kf4
instead, White wins with 59 Kc5
Kg3 60 Kd6 Bc8 61 Kc7! Bh3 62
b5!.

59 b5	axb5+
60 Nxb5+	Ke5
61 Kc5!	Bc8
62 Kb6!	Bh3

Or 62 . . . Kf4 63 Nd6!.

| 63 a6 | Bg2 |
| 64 f4+! | |

White is, of course, interested in
queening the a-pawn for nothing
rather than allow Black's bishop to
sacrifice itself for it. With the ele-
gant text move White deflects
Black's king from d6 and White's
knight can then start to block
Black's bishop from the a-pawn. If
Black now chooses the defensive
64 . . . Ke6, White plays 65 Nd4+,
then Ne2, Ng3, and a7 and either
wins the h-pawn or queens the a-
pawn.

| 64 ... | Kxf4 |
| 65 Nd6 | f5 |

There is no way for Black's
bishop to cope with the a-pawn,
e.g. 65 . . . Ba8 66 Ka7 Bg2 67 Kb8
followed by 68 Nb7.

66 Nb7!	Kg3
67 a7	f4
68 a8=Q	f3
69 Qb8+	
Black resigns	

No. 3. If you passively stand by and allow the opponent to execute his plan, you will lose

I call such passivity "awaiting the
undertaker". There often are situations where the opponent has a very
clear powerful strategic plan and
there is no satisfactory direct way of
preventing it. In such cases, you
must create counterplay in another
part of the board. Otherwise defeat
is assured.

How this happens is shown
from Diagram 60, L. Kavalek –
J. Tarjan, 1978 US Championship,
after Black's 26th move. A quick
look should be sufficient to decide
that Black must be better. Though
material is equal, Black's rook
towers over White's in activity.

(see following diagram)

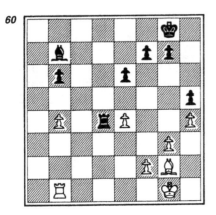

60

White's immediate need is to safe-guard the e-pawn and he does this by:

27 f3!

The correct way. Inferior is 27 e5? Bxg2 28 Kxg2 Kh7 and Black's king has the lovely route of g6 – f5 to get at White's e-pawn. In the meanwhile White's R + K have no prospects for active play.

27 . . .   f5!

It's important for Black to open lines for his bishop.

28 exf5   exf5
29 f4?

A serious strategic error. White is so anxious to prevent the minor threat of 29 . . . f4 that he allows something infinitely worse.

Among the most important strategic principles of endgame play are those involved in simplifying down to a rook endgame. With pawns on one side only or where the defender's rook can be activated, simplification *can* be the right plan in positions a pawn down. Yet paradoxically here, despite material equality, the simplification is wrong for the defending side, because it is *he* who has the passive rook. Of all the pieces, it is the rook which is most affected by its relative activity or passivity. This is because the rook is a powerful attacker, yet a clumsy defender.

White's correct approach was 29 Rb2! safeguarding the second rank and if 29 . . . f4, 30 Kf2. White's disadvantage then is minor, his bishop can be used to keep Black's king out of the light squares on White's side of the board and White has excellent prospects for holding the draw.

29 . . .   Bxg2
30 Kxg2   Kf7
31 Kf2?!

Already on the wrong track. The active 31 Rc1! Rxb4 32 Rc7+ was the best way for getting counter-play.

31 . . .   Ke6

The eye can tell very easily that Black's active K + R gives him a huge advantage. If White does nothing, Black's king will walk over to the queenside and win the b-pawn for nothing.

32 Ke3?

Played much too mechanically. While it is true that in normal endgame positions the king should be centralized, this is hardly a normal position from White's standpoint. It was therefore imperative to activate the rook with 32 Rc1!. After 32 . . . Rxb4 33 Rc6+ White either chases Black's king back to the kingside or captures the g-pawn. In either case White retains fair chances for the draw.

32 . . .	Kd5
33 Rc1?!	

Activity now is fruitless. Therefore the attempt to hold the b-pawn by playing 33 b5 would have been somewhat better.

33 . . .	Rxb4
34 Rc7	g6
35 Rd7+	Kc6
36 Rg7	Re4+
37 Kd3	Re6

Because of his erroneous 29th and 32nd moves, White finds him-

self in the worst of worlds: he has lost his b-pawn and has no prospects against Black's kingside. Black's next order of business is to start advancing his b-pawn.

38 Kd4	b5
39 Rg8	Rd6+
40 Kc3	Kd5
41 Kd3	Kc5+
42 Kc2	Kc4
43 Rc8+	Kd4
44 Re8	Rc6+
45 Kd2	b4
46 Rb8	Kc4
47 Kc2	Ra6!
48 Rc8+	Kd4
49 Rb8	Ra2+
50 Kd1	Rg2

After capturing the b-pawn on move 33, Black has had a theoretically won position. In such cases the tendency is not to give the opponent any practical drawing chances. At this moment Black feels that it's safest to go after White's kingside even at the cost of his b-pawn. The alternative was 50 . . . Kc3 holding the b-pawn for a very easy win. Black didn't want to "risk" losing the g-pawn after 51 Rb6 (or 51 Rc8+ Kb2 52 Rc6), but of course Black's b-pawn would be turned into a new queen.

51 Rxb4+	Ke3
52 Rb3+	Kf2
53 Kd2	Rxg3

| 54 | Rb6 | Rg4 |
| 55 | Re6 | Rxf4 |

Also 55 . . . Kf3 or 55 . . . Kg3 would lead to easy wins. However, Black feels that "safest" is to keep the White king away from the kingside.

56	Rxg6	Rd4+
57	Kc3	Rxh4
58	Rg5	f4
59	Kd3	f3
60	Rf5	Rg4

Entering a theoretically easily won R + P vs R endgame. It almost seems that Black is making things as close as possible. However, totally won positions offer a number of comfortable winning methods.

61	Rxh5	Kg2
62	Rf5	f2
	White resigns	

After 63 Ke2 Re4+ 64 Kd3 Re1 the f-pawn queens.

No. 4. If you open the floodgates, you will lose

Often your opponent is close to executing a successful invasion, but can't quite pull it off. It therefore becomes an absolute must to try to keep him out. If you voluntarily let

him in, you are sure to lose. See what happens from Diagram 61, A. Soltis – J. Tarjan, 1978 US Championship, after Black's 37th move.

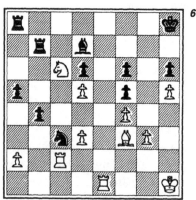
61

A correct evaluation shows that there are lots of similarities: both pawn formations from the d-file to the right are pretty miserable, both bishops are without scope, both knights are already well placed, yet are at the limit of their immediate potential, all the rooks are at their optimal offensive/defensive locations. The only dissimilarity is in Black's favor: he has a sound 2 P vs 1 P Queenside majority. The constraints of the position are such, however, that it is not to be seen how he can generate a passed pawn from his majority. Thus . . . b3 leaves the knight hanging, while a . . . a4 always allows Nxb4, thus again undermining the support of Black's knight. White, on his part also can't undertake anything active since, for instance 38 Re7? is refuted by 38 . . . Bxc6. Over-all Black must be given an edge, because of the theoretical potential behind his queenside pawns. However, careful defense by White should be adequate for the draw. Since it is White to move, a reasonable plan for him is king centralization by 38 Kg2 and 39 Kf2. Instead, under the influence of slight time pressure, he plays the "aggressive":

38 a3??

Handing over to Black on a silver platter something that Black couldn't obtain from his own efforts: a passed queenside pawn.

38 . . .   Na4!

After this simple knight retreat, White is suddenly strategically quite lost.

39	axb4	axb4
40	Rb1	b3
41	Rc4	Nc5
42	Bd1	b2
43	Bc2	Ra1

After White's blunder on move 38, developments have been fast and disastrous for White. Black has run the passed b-pawn down to the 2nd rank and has forced White to defend with R + B to stop it.

44 Kg2

Meekly losing two pawns is chanceless; however, "activity" by 44 Nd8 is zapped by 44 . . . Ba4!, e.g. 45 Rxa4 Nxa4 46 Nxb7 Nc3 etc.

44 . . .		Be8!
45	Kf2	Bxh5
46	Ke1	Bf3
47	Rb4	Rxb4
48	Nxb4	Nb3!

Keeping White's king out of d2 and foiling the unpinning 49 Kf2 by 49 . . . Rxb1 50 Bxb1 Nd2, gaining the bishop for the b-pawn.

49	Nc6	Bxd5
50	Ne7	Be6
51	Ke2	Nd4+
52	Kd2	Kg7!

Black is satisfied to trap and win the strayed knight (53 Rxb2 Ra7!).

53	Kc3	Nxc2
54	Rxb2	Ra7
55	Nc6	Rc7

White resigns

12

Drawing an Inferior Endgame

The two most important general drawing strategies are discussed in this chapter.

Drawing strategy No. 1. Go for counterplay: that is, bring about positions where the opponent has to make decisions

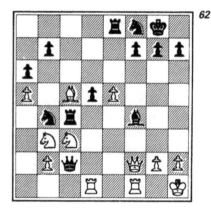

Since perfection in chess is impossible, it is fair to expect that your opponent may not always find all the best moves. Therefore, the key point is to present him with such positions where the correct move is neither simple nor obvious. Make him make some real decisions! A forcing line, where the only correct moves are, in effect "automatic", offers little practical prospects.

The practical execution of the above points are illustrated from Diagram 62, E. Mednis – L. Ljubojevic, Riga Interzonal 1979, after Black's 30th move. White's immediate position is poor,

since he is a pawn down and has no compensation for it. His prospects for the future are equally bleak since the e-pawn will be lost and Black threatens both to exchange queens and play 31 . . . Qxb3.

What to do? 31 Nd2? is unplayable because of 31 . . . Nd3. All forcing lines lead to positions where Black is a pawn up and stands well, e.g. 31 Bxb4 Qxf2 32 Rxf2 Rxb4 33 Nxd5 Rxb3 34 Rxf4 Rxe5 or 31 Qxc2 Nxc2 32 Nxd5 Bxe5. And note that these are forcing lines where it is impossible for Black not to play the correct moves. After using up most of my time—leaving me with about 7 minutes—I decided that the only *practical* try is:

31 Bxf8!   Qxf2

My opponent was rather taken aback by 31 Bxf8, but quite soon "recovered" to play the text.

32 Rxf2

But now Black has to make a fundamental choice regarding how to recapture White's bishop: with the rook, thus "deactivating" the rook or with the king, keeping the rook active? Black now used up most of his remaining time—leaving him with less than 5 minutes – and played . . .

32 . . .   Kxf8?

It is tempting to leave the rook active and attacking the e-pawn, yet it is wrong. After the correct 32 . . . Rxf8! 33 Nxd5 Nxd5 34 Rxd5 Re4 or 34 . . . Re8 Black will in due course come out at least a sound pawn ahead. Admittedly Ljubojevic was in poor sporting form at Riga. Yet the moral is clear: If a world class grandmaster can make a wrong choice—then so can everyone else!

33 Rdf1!

The idea behind White's 31st move: rook activity.

33 . . .   Bxe5
34 Rxf7+   Kg8
35 Rxb7

The immediate result is that White has his pawn back. Though Black appears to still have the more active position and has a strong looking passed d-pawn, White's pieces are well placed both for attack (Rb7) and defense (Rf1, Nc3, Nb3). For instance, 35 . . . d4?! is met by 36 Nd2 Rxc3 37 bxc3 dxc3 38 Nc4! and White—if anyone—is better. Black's next amounts to a slight loss of time, yet the position already is and remains approximately equal.

35 . . .   Rh4
36 h3   Rc4
37 Nd2   Rf4
38 Rxf4!   Bxf4
39 Nf3   Bd6?!

Now Black will be worse. Correct is 39 . . . Rb8! 40 Rd7! with equality.

40 Rd7   Re6
41 Rd8+

The obvious move of course and I made it my sealed move. It is often difficult to decide whether to seal an obvious move or to play it and thus force the opponent to make a decision on the spot. In light of Black's need to play the correct 43rd move, it probably would have been more "practical" for me to "blitz" moves 41–43 in the hope that Black will have to seal at that moment. However, I was already more than happy at the turn of events and didn't want to tempt fate any further.

41 . . .	Bf8
42 Nxd5	Nxd5
43 Rxd5	

White is up a pawn, threatens rook penetration with Rd8/Rd7 and king consolidation with g4. How should Black defend?

| 43 . . . | Rd6!! |

After adjourning I went satisfied back to the hotel and had dinner. At the same table was grandmaster Bent Larsen and he immediately said: "Black's only chances for defending are with 43 . . . Rd6". So it is and it was to be expected that after a night full of analysis the Yusoslav team would find it. The logic of the move is clear: he goes for counterplay, activating his rook while preventing White from doing the same. It is easy to see that 44 Rxd6? is fruitless because White's a- and b-pawns are vulnerable and

Black's king is closer to the center than White's.

44 Rd4!

White threatens to consolidate his king position with 45 g4 while starting to centralize it thereafter with Kg2. 44 . . . Rxd4? does not satisfy Black because of 45 Nxd4 Kf7 46 Nc6 Bd6 47 b4 Ke6 48 b5 Kd5 49 Na7!.

| 44 . . . | Kf7! |

Centralizing the king. If now 45 g4?! Rxd4 46 Nxd4 Bd6 and White, being a "knight move" behind the previous line, has less than nothing.

45 Rf4+

Expecting/hoping for 45 . . . Ke8?! and White with 46 Re4 *check* gains the necessary tempo to consolidate and thereby retains good winning chances.

| 45 . . . | Kg8!! |

Prevents White from consolidating (46 Re4? Rd1+ 47 Kh2 Bd6+ etc.). There is nothing better than to repeat the position.

46 Rd4	Kf7
47 Rf4+	Kg8
Draw	

Drawing strategy No. 2. Protect your vulnerable point(s) in such a way that you can combine smooth defense with chances for counterplay

It shouldn't be difficult to see that in Diagram 63, K. Regan – P. Benko, 1978 US Championship after Black's 21st move, it is White who must be better. He has all of

63

his forces effectively trained on the chronic weakness in Black's position, the e-pawn. Black on the other hand is in no position to get at White's only weakness, the c-pawn. White's next logical step should be to fix Black's e-pawn by playing 22 g3! and 23 f4. Black can't prevent this by 22 . . . Rf3? because of the following tactical refutation: 23 Rxe6! Rxe6 24 Rxe6! Rxc3 25 Rxb6+! Rxc4 26 Rxb7+ followed

by 27 Rxa7 and White is up two pawns. Therefore after 22 g3! Black would probably respond as in the game with 22 . . . Re7 and after 23 f4 he should most likely prevent the possible 24 f5 by the defensive 23 . . . g6. Nevertheless, White's advantage is obvious to the eye: he has strong pressure against Black's position as well as the inherently superior bishop. Yet instead of the consistent 22 g3! White continued with:

22 a4?!

Completely misreading the field of action. The aim of exchanging off the a-pawn has little strategic meaning because there was nothing wrong with the a-pawn. If White could trade his c-pawn for Black's b-pawn, that would be a worthwhile accomplishment.

22 . . .	**Re7!**
23 a5	**Bc8!**

By protecting his e-pawn with the bishop, Black frees his rook for action along the c-file.

24 R1e3?!

By playing without sufficient strategic regard for the position, White quickly goes from a clearly superior position to one where he must scratch for a draw. Correct was the obvious 24 axb6 with total equality.

24 ...   Rc7
25 Bb3   bxa5!

This thoughtful exchange yields Black the outside passed pawn—something to look forward to in the future.

26 Rxa5   Kf8!

By getting out of the pin on the e-pawn, Black prepares the coming rook move, thus activating his other rook.

27 Kf1   Rf5
28 Rxf5+?!

Why straighten out Black's pawn formation? Correct was the retreat 28 Ra3 with virtual equality.

28 ...   exf5
29 Ke2   f4
30 Re4   g5
31 Kd2   Rd7+
32 Kc2   Bb7
33 Re5   h6
34 g3   Re7!
35 Rxe7   Kxe7

Black has a slight advantage due to having the outside passed pawn. Since *this theme is not important for this chaper*, I shall give the rest of the game without further comments.

36 Kd3   fxg3
37 fxg3   Kf6?
38 Kd4   Bf3
39 c4?   Ke6!
40 Ba4?!   Kd6
41 c5+   Kc7
42 Kc4   Bc6
43 Bd1   a5!
44 Bg4   Kd8!
45 h4!   Ke7
46 hxg5   hxg5
47 Kd4   Kf6
48 Bh5   Kf5
49 Bd1   a4!
50 Kc3   a3
51 Bb3!   Ke5
52 Kb4   Kd4
53 Kxa3   Kxc5
54 Kb2   Kd4
55 Kc1   Ke3
56 Be6   Bf3
57 Bd7   Kf2
58 Kd2!   Kxg3
59 Ke1   Bg2
60 Be6   Kh2
61 Bg4!
Draw

13

Drawing an Inferior Endgame – Grand Strategy

In the previous chapter I discussed the two most basic principles in trying to draw inferior endgames: going for counterplay and defending weak points in such a manner as to also offer opportunities for counterplay. Here I will expand on these principles and will demonstrate how the application of the various principles can be successfully combined.

The overriding theme of the example discussed is the need and value of always understanding the correct defensive plan. Diagram 64 is E. Mednis–O. Romanishin, Riga Interzonal 1979, after Black's 32nd move. This relatively unbalanced position arose after a somewhat forced series of pawn and piece exchanges. The more I looked at this position, the less I liked it. All of Black's pieces stand very well —both for offensive and defensive purposes—whereas White's knight is under attack and has no attractive square to go to. Most importantly,

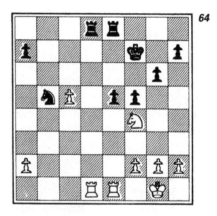

64

White's c-pawn is weak and extremely vulnerable to being captured. What to do? Unfortunately 33 Rxd8?! Rxd8 34 Rxe5?? allows mate and 33 Nd5?! puts the Knight in a clearly unstable position. After considerable thought, I played:

33 Ne2!

White's first need is to keep Black's knight out of c3, where it would be very powerful. Therefore unsatisfactory is 33 Nd3? Nc3 34 Rd2. Romanishin provides the following convincing line: 34 . . . Kg7! (Preventing a Ne5 with *check*.) 35 c6 e4! 36 c7 exd3! and because of the mate threat on the first rank Black has won a piece.

33 . . .   Nc7!

To go after the c-pawn with . . . Ne6.

34 Rb1!?

Here and in the following moves White tries to set up a defense of his c-pawn so as to leave some chances for active play. Black, in the meanwhile, goes straight for the pawn.

34 . . .	**Ne6**
35 c6	**Re7**
36 Rec1	**Rc7**
37 Rc4	**Rd6**

Despite what can be clearly termed White's best efforts his situation remains bleak. After 38 Rb7?? Black has the "choice" between mate and winning the c-pawn with 38 . . . Rdxc6; after 38 Rbc1, 38 . . . Nd8 wins the pawn. In the latter case Black wins the pawn without risk and in a very favourable over-all position, i.e. Black keeps his strong central e-pawn and his king is closer to the centre than White's.

Since three moves still remained before time control and Black didn't have enough time left for deep thinking, I decided on a bold plan.

38 f4!?

Forcing Black to make a *major* decision *before* time control. This is always a key approach in trying to draw inferior endgames. Chess is a difficult game and in complicated positions it is always possible to make a wrong move, especially so when the time available for the decision is short. The strategic point of the move is that after 38 . . . e4 the d4 square can become accessible to White's knight, thus enhancing White's chances for holding his well advanced passed c-pawn. After the game Romanishin told me that he didn't play 38 . . . e4 because "I was afraid that I then won't be able to win the c-pawn." Note that this kind of "natural" feeling comes from one of the top players in the world. Therefore, it can very easily come from anyone else, too.

38 . . .   exf4?!

It could be helpful to set the external conditions under which this game was played. This was the next to last round and Romanishin needed a win to stay in contention for the third and last qualifying spot for the Candidates Matches (As it subsequently turned out, he was exactly half a point short.) So a win is imperative and a loss is disastrous yet in a strict sense—as far as third place is concerned—little worse than a draw. Still, under these circumstances, Black decides on a "bird in hand" (a clear pawn advantage in a R + P endgame) over the possible bounty "in the bush" after 38 . . . e4 (protected passed e-pawn, vulnerable white c- and f-pawns). We'll discuss in a moment why the "bird in the hand" is the insufficient plan.

Subsequent analysis showed that 38 . . . e4! would have led to a winning position for Black. After 39 Rbc1 Rd2! Romanishin gives the following two variations: (1) 40 R4c2 Rxc2 41 Rxc2 Ke7 and the coming . . . Kd6 will win the c-pawn, while of course retaining the protected passed e-pawn, (2) 40 Nc3 a6! and White's counterplay is stopped while the various weaknesses in his position remain.

39 Nxf4	**Nxf4**
40 Rxf4	**Rdxc6**
41 Ra4!	(Diagram 65)

It may appear that Black has won a pawn for nothing, but is it really "nothing"? Of course, Black cannot *lose* this position, but as far as drawing chances are concerned, White has made several giant steps

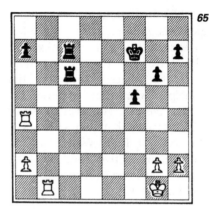

forward. Most importantly, White has been able to exchange off Black's valuable e-pawn for his own f-pawn. The resulting kingside formation is a normal 3 P vs 2 P situation, which is perfectly fine for defensive purposes. It also is in White's interest to have exchanged off the knights since this lessens Black's attacking power. The corollary here is that only rooks are left on the board and R + P endgames are notorious for giving excellent drawing chances to a well-placed defender.

With his last move White achieves a double purpose: the rook smoothly protects his own a-pawn while attacking Black's a-pawn. Thus this rook is excellently placed. Looking at the whole White position we can see that there is nothing wrong with it except of course that he is down a normal kingside pawn.

41 . . .   Rc2

Black had another major strategic decision to make here: whether to exchange a pair of rooks with 41 . . . Rc1+ 42 Rxc1 Rxc1+. This would be in accordance with the principle "when ahead material, exchange pieces". However, it is not difficult to see that after 43 Kf2 Rc7 (Forced) 44 Ra6! White has the much more active rook, making Black's winning prospects most problematical.

42 h3!

Since White's other rook wants to leave the first rank, the king needs a comfortable hiding place.

42 . . .   Rd7
43 Rb3!

White also places this rook so that it can combine defensive functions (Rg3 to protect the g-pawn) with offensive prospects (Rba3 attacking the a-pawn). Here the game was adjourned with Black sealing his move. After dinner, Tarjan's and my second, World Junior Champion (and now Grandmaster) Yasser Seirawan, and I spent a couple of hours analyzing. He then had to leave to also assist Jim Tarjan in his analysis. I went to bed early satisfied that I had found no forced winning plan for Black.

Next morning at breakfast Yasser told me that he's sorry to say so, but that he is certain that I must be lost, because "White just can't get any counterplay". Though not happy to hear his evaluation, I still felt confident because I didn't see *how Black can make decisive progress*—and after all, I wasn't interested in a win, but just a draw! (After the game Romanishin told me that he and his second, International master Arshak Petrosian, had also not found a forced win.)

43 . . .   Kf6

I had rather expected 43 . . . Kg7 after which the only correct move is 44 Rg3! so that after 44 . . . Kh6 White can chase Black's king back with 45 Rh4+.

44 Rg3!

The key defensive plan that I had discovered in my analysis is that Black's king must be prevented from getting to h5. At that location the king would be safe from White's rooks and could participate in a decisive attack on White's king. The kind of position that always was hopeless for White is: Black's rooks on c2 and d2, Black king on h5, Black's pawns on f4, g5, h6. With the text move, Black's king is kept out of g5.

44 . . .   Re2

The immediate attempt at action with 44 . . . a5 45 Rxa5 Rd1+ 46 Kh2 f4 (threatening 47 . . . Rcc1) is defended against by 47 Ra6+! Kg7 48 Rg4 f3 (or 48 . . . Rdd2 49 Kh1!) 49 Ra7+ Kg8 (49 . . . Kh6 50 Rh4+ Kg5 51 Rg4+) 50 Ra8+! etc.

45 Kh2   Kg7
46 Kg1!

White's rooks are at their optimal locations so that keeping the status quo with king moves is the right approach.

46 . . .   Rb2
47 Kh2   Rc2
48 Kg1   Kh6
49 Kh4+!

Black's king must be kept away from h5.

49 . . .   Kg7
50 Ra4!

Mission accomplished. What now Black?

50 . . .   a5?!

One of the specific problems in Black's position is that the a-pawn is on the 7th rank and White can capture it there under favorable (such as with check) circumstances. This ties down one of Black's rooks to its defense. If Black attacks with

50 . . . Rdd2, White can defend with 51 Rxa7+ Kh6 52 Raa3!, e.g. 52 . . . f4 53 Rg4 g5 54 h4!.

Therefore, prior to doubling rooks Black wants to put his a-pawn on a less unfavourable square. But because of the tactical possibility shown in the note to White's 53rd move, a5 has a specific problem. Better therefore is 50 . . . a6!?. Subsequent analysis showed the following line as best for both sides: 51 Rxa6 f4 52 Rf3! Rdd2 53 Ra7+Kh6 54 Rxf4 Rxg2+ 55 Kh1! Rh2+56 Kg1 Rxh3 57 Rff7! followed by 58 Rxh7. Black then has a very active position but has only one pawn remaining. The position is complicated and unclear, but White should have good chances for the draw.

51 Rxa5!   f4
52 Rf3!

Both rooks must be employed in a smooth defensive combination.

52 . . .   Rdd2
53 Rg5   (Diagram 66)

(see following diagram)

White now has a draw because Black cannot fortify his kingside pawns. The specific problem is that 53 . . . h6 54 Rg4 g5 allows 55 Rfxf4!.

66

| 53 . . . | Kf6 |
| 54 h4! | |

But not 54 Rg4? g5 55 h4 h6. After the text 54 . . . h6? fails to the obvious 55 Rxf4+.

54 . . .	Rc4
55 Rg4	Kf5
56 Rg5+	Kf6

After 56 . . . Ke4 White again plays 57 Rg4.

| 57 Rg4 | Rdd4 |
| 58 g3! | |

The even exchange of White's g-pawn for Black's f-pawn ensures White a theoretically and practically drawn R + P endgame.

58 . . .	Rd1+
59 Rf1!	Rxf1+
60 Kxf1	Rc1+
61 Kg2	Rc2+
62 Kh3	fxg3
63 a4!	

There is no reason to give Black the a-pawn, even though the endgame remains quite drawn. Here I offered a draw, which Black mostly out of inertia, I guess, refused.

63 . . .	h5
64 Rxg3	Ra2
65 Rf3+	Draw

Offered by Black. After 65 . . . Ke5 66 Rg3 or 65 . . . Kg7 66 Rf4 neither side has the slightest advantage.

14

Stalemate in Queen Endgames

You find yourself in an inferior endgame involving queen(s). A draw is the best that you can hope for. How to achieve a draw by utilizing stalemate is the subject of this chapter. I shall first give the basic principles and then show how these can be applied in practical situations.

Because the queen is so powerful, it is exactly queen endgames which offer the best chances for stalemate draws. The queen can wind up controlling so many squares that the enemy king simply has nowhere to go. The two most basic positions are illustrated in Diagram 67. With White's king on h1, it doesn't matter whether Black's queen is on f2 or g3—in either case White has been stalemated.

The above positions are the basis for the rule that in the endgame of passed pawn on the 7th rank vs. queen, bishop and rook pawns draw, if supported by own king and the enemy king is far away. The key

position with a bishop pawn is shown in Diagram 68. If White

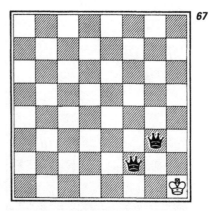

67

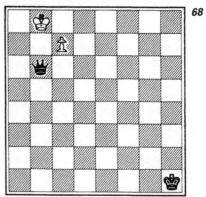

68

would have to protect his pawn with Kc8, Black would have time to start moving his king closer with Kg2. But White simply plays:

1 Ka8!
Draw

1 . . . Qxc7 is stalemate and Black has no other reasonable plan.

The key position with a rook pawn is shown in Diagram 69. Here White has the best of both worlds,

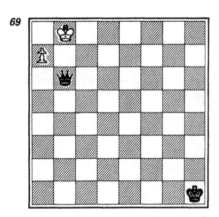

69

because the containing nature of the rook pawn allows White to set up a stalemate position while protecting his pawn. White plays:

1 Ka8!
Draw

Notice that the correct stalemate move is to the corner. We have stalemate as long as Black's queen

remains on the b-file and also of no help is 1 . . . Qc7 (planning 2 Qc8 mate) because White again has been stalemated.

Now we are ready to start executing these ideas. A typical case is Diagram 70, P. Atanasov – Spiridonov, Ruse 1978, Black to move. He is two pawns down and chances for

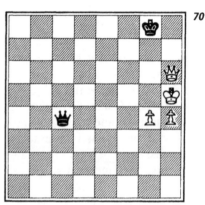

70

a perpetual check are nil. Yet there is a draw by utilizing stalemate motifs:

1 . . .   Qf7+!!

Seems suicidal because White has:

2 Qg6+

There is nothing better since 2 Kg5 Qd5+! 3 Kf6 (3 Kf4?? Qd2+) 3 . . . Qe6+! again gives White only the choice of acquiescing to a draw via stalemate or perpetual check.

2 ...   Kh8!
3 Kg5

After 3 Kh6 Black re-establishes the status quo with 3 . . . Qf8+! 4 Kh5 Qf7!.

3 . . .   Qf4+!!
Draw

4 Kxf4 is stalemate; 4 Kh5 Qf7! is repetition.

Consider now Diagram 71, Nesis – Kolker, USSR Correspondence Championship, 1977/78, after

71
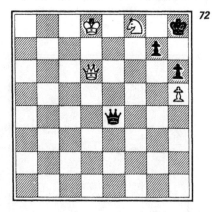

White's 46th move. Black's prospects look bleak: with his queen relegated to protecting the back rank, what is to prevent White from marching the c-pawn up the board? However, there is also a positive side to Black's king containment: he is so contained that his only access is to g8. Now if only that square could also be "given" to White . . .

46 . . .   Qg8!!
Draw agreed!

White's c-pawn is momentarily pinned and next move will come the drawing 47 . . . Qxc4!! since 48 Qxc4 is stalemate.

The creative execution of a similar concept allows Black to salvage a draw from Diagram 72, Semeniuk – Timoshchenko, USSR 1978, after

72
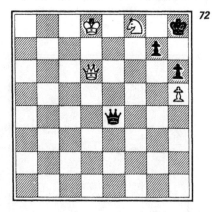

Black's 61st move. For quite some time White had been floundering around with the extra piece. Being short of time now, a "protect everything" move such as 62 Qc5! is well in order. Instead:

62 Qg6?

Why not go for Black's throat to get the game over as quickly as possible? This is what White must have thought—but what happens is different from what he intended!

62 . . .	**Qa8+**
63 Ke7	**Qxf8+!**
Draw	

After 64 Kxf8 Black has been stalemated.

When the king is contained in the corner, there are always *some* stalemate chances. Diagram 73, with White to move, is from an interesting analysis of a knight endgame, as published by Grandmaster Holmov in *Shahmaty Biulletin*, No. 3, 1977.

73

White's far advanced c-pawn, supported by his king, does give White the clearly superior chances. Yet Black's h-pawn is nothing to be

sneezed at either. In fact White only has one way of winning:

1 Nc3?

This is not it, because White must not only queen but do so with check. Correct is 1 Nd4! h4 2 Nc6! h3 3 Nd8+ Ka7 4 Kxc8 h2 5 Nc6+ Ka8 6 Kd7 followed by 7 c8=Q Mate.

1 . . .	**h4**
2 Ne4	**h3!**
3 Nc5+	**Ka7**
4 Kxc8	**h2**
5 Kd8	**h1=Q**
6 c8=Q	

Note that Black's king has been stalemated. Therefore:

6 . . .	**Qh8+**
7 Kd7	**Qd8+!!**
Draw	

No matter how White captures, it's stalemate!

Our basic "king in the corner" stalemate is beautifully exploited from Diagram 74, a 1950 study by

(see following diagram)

V. Halberstadt. In this kind of pawnless position, R + B are enough to draw against the queen, if none of them are lost. Unfortunately something has to give here.

74

However, the "bad" position of White's king is good enough for artistic stalemate play:

1 Be1!

It is easy enough to see that the rook has no safe square on the 5th rank. The immediate point of the text move is easy enough to see: 1 . . . Qxc5 2 Bf2! Qxf2 stalemate. But Black can make things more difficult with . . .

1 . . .	Qe3!
2 Bg3!!	

The tempting 2 Bf2? fails to 2 . . . Qxf2 3 Ra5+ (or 3 Rc7+ Ka6! 4 Rc6+ Kb5!) 3 . . . Kb7! 4 Rb5+ Kc6! and White's checks are over since after either 5 Rb6+ or 5 Rc5+ Black can recapture with the queen.

| 2 . . . | Qxg3 |

Or 2. . . Kb6 3 Rc2! Qxg3 4 Rb2+, with a perpetual check on the second rank. Note that if Black's king goes to the f-file, White always has Rf2+ and if Black's king reaches the g-file, White pins Black's queen with Rg2.

3 Ra5+	Kb6
4 Ra6+	Kc5
5 Ra5+	Kd6
6 Ra6+	Ke5
7 Ra5+	Kf6
8 Ra6+	Kf5
9 Ra5+!	Kf4
10 Ra4+!	Kg5
11 Ra5+	

White checks along the a-file until Black's king reaches the g- or h- file and then:

11 . . .	Kh4
12 Rh5+!!	Kg4
13 Rg5+	Kxg5
Stalemate	

So far the stalemates have occurred in the corner. This is the most popular place. Yet anywhere along the *edge* of the board is often good enough. Paying insufficient attention to such a possibility can rob White of a win from Diagram 75. It

(see following diagram)

is White's move, of course, and let us see how he can *not* win:

1 Kg4

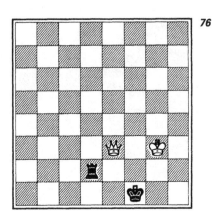

Simpler is 1 Kg5! Qg3+ 2 Qg4.

1 . . .   Qg1+
2 Kh3?

Either 2 Kf5 or 2 Kh5 does win.
But after the text isn't Black immediately out of checks? The
answer is "No"!

2 . . .   Qe3+!!
3 Qxe3
Stalemate

The above stalemate position is
important. Knowledge of it would
have allowed Black to draw from
Diagram 76, which occurred after
White's 75th move in a game between two unnamed players in Seat-
tle (USA) 1980. Black was to seal
his move here and it should have
been:

75 . . .   Rg2+

Instead   Black   sealed
75 . . . Ra2?? and lost.

76 Kh3

After 76 Kf3 Black draws with
76 . . . Rg3+!!; 76 Kf4 Rf2+ leads
to a perpetual check along the g-
and h- files since White can never
cross the e-file because of . . . Re2.

76 . . .   Rh2+!!
77 Kxh2
Stalemate

The *only* real requirement for a
stalemate is that the king be contained. In Diagram 77, Dikarev –

(see following diagram)

Peltz, 1964 Ukrainian Championship, White to move, the presence
of White's h-pawn is containment
enough:

77

1 Qe5+!   Qg7

Or 1 . . . Kh7 2 Qg7+!!

2 Qb8+!!   Qxb8
Stalemate

In Diagram 78, L. Vogt – B. Gulko, Cienfuegos 1976, after White's 55th move, we see that White has succeeded in building a marvelous contained castle for his

king. This allows him to achieve a draw as follows:

55 . . .	b2
56 Qe8+	Kc7
57 Qe7+	Kb6
58 Qd6+	Kb5
59 Qd1!!	

Finally disclosing his plan: 59 . . . Qxd1 is stalemate, as is 59 . . . b1=Q 60 Qxb1+! Qxb1.

| 59 . . . | Qc1! |

A bit of a trap: after 60 Qxc1? Black wins with 60 . . . bxc1=B or 60 . . . bxc1=N.

60 Qb3+	Kc5
61 Qd5+!	
Draw	

Black sees that he must either allow perpetual check or stalemate.

For my last example I want to present Diagram 79, Z. Solmanis –

78

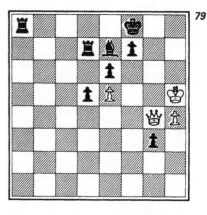

79

Remmel, Riga 1979, after Black's 43rd move. Though not strictly a queen endgame, it is a perfect demonstration of the attitude necessary to save lost positions by achieving stalemate. Black's position is of course totally won. He is clearly ahead on material, has an unstoppable passed d-pawn and no worries whatever. If White would resign here, I would think that it is quite a proper thing to do. Yet White spies a creative swindling chance and feels that it is worth a last try:

44 Kh6!   d4

White is perhaps planning an attack with Qg7+? Well, that's no problem!

45 h5!

Ah, White is planning an advance of the h-pawn?

45 . . .   d3??

Clearly that is nothing to worry about! (Winning is, for instance, 45 . . . Ke8).

46 Qg8+!!

Ouch, ouch, ouch! White was planning stalemate!

46 . . .   Kxg8
Stalemate

And so on this note I end our little excursion to stalemates in queen endgames. Learn the basic principles and then use your own creativity in trying to apply them in your own games.

15

Stalemate in King + Pawn Endgames

The single most important position in K + P vs. K endgames is the type shown in Diagram 80. It is drawn if *White is to move*. Its importance derives from the fact that if the defensive king is immediately in front of the pawn (e.g. White: Ke4, e5; Black: Ke6), then it can always reach Diagram 80 with the opponent on move. The discussion of Diagram 80 generally emphasizes the importance of the concept of opposition, i.e. Black draws here because he has the opposition. This

is quite true, of course. Still, I want the reader to follow the thematic play to come:

1 e7+	**Ke8**
2 Ke6	**Stalemate!**

Thus the actual drawing resource was stalemate and opposition was just the method to achieve this. *The purpose of this chapter is to get the reader to always think of the possibility of achieving stalemate as a way of saving inferior K + P endgames.*

The stalemates resulting from Diagram 80 type position are equally valid for all eight pawns. For rook pawns—since they are the worst ones to have for direct queening purposes in K + P endgames—there is another fully satisfactory defensive king position. With White's king in front of his pawn, if the black king can get to c7 when White has an a-pawn (or to f7 for the h-pawn), then the position is drawn, irrespective of the exact location of White's king.

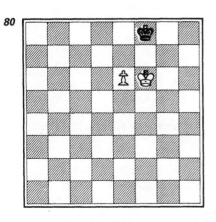

80

This—as well as another important point—is well illustrated from Diagram 81, an instructive study by Grigoriev. Even though White is to move, he seems to be in serious trouble since Black will win White's a-pawn while simultaneously protecting his own. However, we are dealing with rook pawns and have learned above that if White's king can get to c2 immediately after Black has captured on a2, then the position is drawn. But how to achieve this?

81

To make the search for the correct method easier, it is useful to introduce the following principle regarding king movements: *on an open board, all routes are equally fast in going from one point to another.* In our specific position White's king wants to get to c2. A direct vertical route along the c-file takes six moves. A strictly diagonal route (e.g. Kb7–a6–b5–c4–d3–c2) also takes six moves. Try a combination of rectangular and diagonal steps: Kd7–d6–c5–c4–b3–c2— again six moves!

Unfortunately, because of the presence of Black's king, White's cannot utilize the c7 square. Therefore another route is necessary. Let's try the following one: 1 Kd7 Kc5 2 Ke6 Kd4 3 Kd6 Kc3 4 Kc5 Kb2 5 Kb4 Kxa2 6 Kc3 Kb1 — but Black wins. What went wrong? Well, Black's king got to b2 in the minimum of four moves. However, White's king—because of interference by Black's king—could not reach c2 in the required six moves. Therefore, what White needs is a six-move route with which Black's king cannot interfere. This is the way:

1 Kd7	Kc5
2 Ke6	Kd4!
3 Kf5!	

Instead of 3 Kd6?.

3 . . .	Kc3
4 Ke4	Kb2
5 Kd3	Kxa2
6 Kc2!	

Success in six moves! The rest is easy.

6 . . .	Ka1
7 Kc1	a2
8 Kc2	Stalemate

It is actually the offensive king who gets stalemated in this case!

The stalemate of Diagram 81 is of recurring importance in practical play. Witness how White saves himself from Diagram 82, Kasimov–Komay, Israel 1979, Black to move.

82

White's rook is stuck on h1 to prevent the pawn(s) from queening and what is to prevent Black's king from decisively infiltrating into White's position? Yet White achieves a thematic stalemate draw as follows:

1 . . .	Ke5
2 Kc5	Kxe4
3 Kc4!	Ke3
4 Kc3!	

Losing is 4 Kd5? Kf3 5 Kd4 Kg2 6 Ke3 f1=Q!

4 . . .	Kf3

It is no good going to the e-file, since 4 . . . Ke2 allows 5 Rxh2 and the f-pawn is pinned.

5 Kd3	Kg2
6 Ke2!!	Draw

After 6 . . . Kxh1 White stalemates Black with the normal 7 Kxf2 or the "fancy" 7 Kf1.

As a general observation, the more contained the king is, the better its chances are for stalemate. A characteristic situation is shown in Diagram 83. Because Black's king is so contained, it has no chance to resist the advance of White's king by establishing opposition. However, Black saves the game easily because of stalemate. It doesn't matter whose move it is. If it is White's, play could be:

1 Kd8	Kg8
2 Ke8	Kh8
3 Kf8	Stalemate

83

As a matter of fact, Black's king is so contained in Diagram 83 that even if White is given a light square bishop, there is still no win. White can then stalemate Black in many many ways, but there is no mate!

Because of the containing nature of the pawn structure of Diagram 83, similar positions with a one-pawn advantage may not be won either. For example: White: Ke6, g6, h5; Black: Kg7, h6 is drawn irrrespective of who is to move. Again White only has the frustrating choice of which stalemate to allow.

The process of gaining a stalemate draw because of the contained king is shown from Diagram 84,

84

J. Mestel–Sznapik, Buenos Aires Olympiad 1978, White to move. On the face of it, Diagram 84 should illustrate the principle that the out-

side passed pawn is a winning advantage in K + P endgames. Well, White can and does win *a* pawn, but not *the game*:

1 b4	Kc6
2 Ke5	Kb5
3 Kxd5	Kxb4
4 Ke5	

White can win the h-pawn with 4 Ke6, but then Black saves himself with the method from Diagram 81: 4 ... Kc5! 5 Kf7 Kd6 6 Kg7 Ke7 7 Kxh7 Kf7! 8 Kh8 Kf8!. Then 9 h7?? Kf7 even loses for White because of the presence of the other pawns. Thus White has nothing better than to repeat the position with 9 Kh7 Kf7 etc.

4 ...	Kc5
5 Kxf4	Kd4
6 Kg5	Ke5
7 g3	Ke6
8 Kf4	Kf6
9 Ke4	Ke6!

Black's draw will come from the fortunate "containing" character of the pawn formation. Therefore the last thing that he wants to do is touch his g-pawn. Losing is 9 ... g5? 10 Kd5! Kg6 (10 ... Kf5 11 Kd6! Kf6 12 g4) 11 Ke6 Kxh6 12 Kf6 Kh5 13 Kg7! g4 (13 ... h6 14 g4+) 14 f4 h6 15 f5 and the f-pawn queens.

10	Kd4	Kd6
11	Kc4	Kc6
12	f4	Kd6
13	g4	Ke6
14	Kc3	Ke7
15	Kd4	Kf6
16	Kc5	Ke7
17	Kd5	Kf7
18	Ke4	Ke6
19	Kf3	

Over the last several moves and during the next few, White is moving around with his king since pawn advances do not work. Thus 19 f5+ gxf5+ 20 gxf5+ Kf6 20 Kf4 Kf7 will only lead to the Diagram 80 type of stalemate draw. (The presence of the h-pawns in this case is immaterial.)

19	. . .	Kf7
20	Kg3	Ke7
21	Kf2	Kf6
22	Ke3	Ke7
23	Kd4	Kf6
24	Kd5	Kf7
25	Kd6	Kf6
26	Kd7	Kf7
27	g5	

The game was called a draw after 27 f5 gxf5 28 gxf5 Kf6, because of 29 Ke8 Kxf5 30 Kf7 Ke5! 31 Kg7 Ke6 32 Kxh7 Kf7—Diagram 81 again.

27	. . .	Kf8
28	Ke6	Kg8!

Heading for containment! Losing is 28 . . . Ke8? because of 29 f5! gxf5 30 g6!.

29 f5

Or 29 Ke7 Kh8 30 Kf7 Stalemate— the diagram 83 type.

29	. . .	gxf5
30	Kxf5	Kh8!
31	Kf6	Kg8
32	Ke7	Kh8
33	Kf7	Stalemate

Pawn up endgames, where a rook pawn is part of the pawn formation, offer considerably less winning chances than formations without a rook's pawn. The two reasons for this are: (1) the rook's pawn as the last remaining pawn may not be promotable, and (2) the chances for a stalemate defense are considerably increased. The play from Diagram 84 has already illustrated some of the above problems. Therefore, I want to warn the superior side to be extremely wary about voluntarily heading for such endgames. True, they are won part of the time, but they also lead to draws much too often for comfort. Witness what happens from Diagram 85, J. Tarjan–B. Larsen,

(see following diagram)

Riga Interzonal 1979, after White's 68th move. Black is up a sound

85

passed f-pawn, has an over-all excellent position and very good winning chances in the R + P endgame. Yet he erroneously forces a drawn K + P endgame by playing:

68 ...	Rh4?
69 Rxh4	gxh4
70 Kf4	f5
71 Ke3!	

For connoisseurs of this type of endgame, it can be pointed out that it is lost for White if his h-pawn is already on h3. Therefore here too, losing is the unmotivated 71 h3?.

71 ...	Kf7
72 Kf3	Ke6
73 Kf4	Kf6
74 Ke3	Ke5
75 Kf3	f4
76 Ke2!	

The key to successful defense is stalemate, not king activity! There-

fore, 76 Kg4? Ke4 77 Kxh4 f3 wins the h-pawn but loses the game.

76 ...	Ke4
77 Kf2	f3
78 Ke1!	

White must time his king moves so that his king is stalemated at the same time that his h-pawn has no moves. Incorrect is 78 Kf1? Ke3 79 Ke1 f2+ 80 Kf1 Kf3 81 h3 Kg3 and Black wins.

| 78 ... | Ke3 |
| 79 Kf1 | f2 |

An alternate stalemate results after 79 ... h3 80 Ke1 f2+ 81 Kf1 Kf3.

| 80 h3 | Kf3 |
| Stalemate | |

The relatively slight level of king containment was sufficient to draw in the above example. With the king more contained, there are positions which appear to be much worse, but allow the saving defense based on stalemate. This is well demonstrated from Diagram 86,

(see following diagram)

Zidkov–Grohotov, USSR 1976, Black on move. White has the passive king and Black can force a protected passed pawn—yet there is no win:

86

It's stalemate after 5 . . . f2, with Black's h-pawn being the culprit. And Black has no other way of trying to make progress.

No matter how bleak the outlook try to see if there is a chance for a surprising stalemate. Sometimes there is! This discussion brings me back to thinking about my early tournament days and specifically about the position of Diagram 87, N. Aronson–E. Mednis,

1 . . .   f4

Without this break there is no way of making progress. White can't capture since 2 gxf4? g3! wins for Black.

2 Kd2   Ke4
3 Ke1!

White still wants to avoid the capture as that would allow Black an eventual break with . . . g3, in combination with king penetration into White's kingside.

3 . . .   fxg3

After 3 . . . Kd3 4 Kf1, impossible is 4 . . . Kd2?? because of 5 gxf4.

4 fxg3   Ke3
5 Kf1   Draw

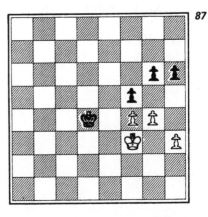

87

US Open 1953, after Black's 52nd move. For a long time I had a winning ending with an extra pawn, but then suddenly had decided to give it back to "simplify" into the "winning" K + P endgame of Diagram 87. As I started to look deeper into it, I saw that it is not winning at all. So I got up and walked around a bit. Some of my friends came up and already congratulated me on a fine win. But all I could say was a cheerless "It's not so simple." the drawing line is:

53 g5!

In the game White played the routine 53 h4? and lost after 53 . . . h5! 54 gxf5 gxf5 55 Kf2 Ke4 56 Kg3 Ke3 etc.

53 . . .   h5

There also is nothing in 53 . . . hxg5 54 fxg5 Ke5 55 h4 f4 56 h5! gxh5 57 g6 Kf6 58 Kxf4 Kxg6 59 Kg3.

54 Kg3!!	Ke3
55 Kh4!!	Kxf4
Stalemate	

So it can be said that Black was lucky to win. Yet the reason for White's loss is absolutely clear: unless you search for miracles, you won't find them.

Part IV

General Strategies of Exchanging Queens in the Middlegame

The book up to now has concentrated on endgame play and I have
demonstrated how to handle the various types of endgames — be they
equal, superior or inferior. Now it is time to consider the second important
theme of this book: when should we *voluntarily* enter the endgame. The
single most dramatic exchange is that of the queens, and this is the moment
that I shall use as the transition from the middlegame into the endgame. Of
course, we have learned already in Chapter 1 that this "rule" should not be
followed blindly. Still, in the vast majority of cases the exchange of queens
does bring about an endgame and, in all cases, this exchange leads to a very
major change in the position. Thus, both for practical and pedagogical
reasons, it seems proper to use the exchange of queens as a proxy for
passing from the middlegame into the endgame.

Whenever you are thinking about exchanging queens, there are a
number of general points and principles to keep in mind. These are
presented in Chapters 16, 17 and 18. With this background we are ready to
start discussing the three kinds of middlegames: equal, superior and
inferior. It is easiest to apply the techniques discussed to equal middlegames and therefore, in Chapter 19, I start with these.

16

Exchanging Queens on Your Terms

You want to be as successful as possible in every game you play. This requires the habit of concentrating every moment. It requires paying attention to *every* detail. The grandmaster knows that to win he will have to accumulate a lot of small advantages. In the language of American football this means grinding out lots of yards on the ground. His opponent, a fellow grandmaster, will not give anything way. Again in football talk: he will not allow the deep pass to be completed. Therefore, you, too, must become accustomed to playing long and hard to gain the win from superior positions and hold inferior positions for a draw.

Success requires to both come up with the correct plan *and then to execute it in the most accurate way.* As appropriate for the subject of this chapter, suppose that you have decided — quite correctly — that you want to exchange queens. The next important objective is to achieve this in the most favorable manner.

Of course, you never want to make your situation worse. A perfect example of what not to do is shown from Diagram 88, G. Sax – S. Kindermann, Plovdiv 1983, after White's 28th move. Black has two strategic advantages: the superior center and the potentially more active bishop. Yet obviously enough, the strong attack White's queen + rook have against Black's king makes it impossible for Black

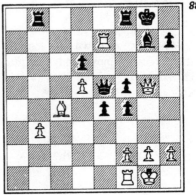

88

to capitalize on these factors. Therefore, quite correctly, Black is happy to exchange queens:

28 . . .   Qf6!

White must exchange since if he moves the queen, the rook is left *en prise*. Normal and in order now is 29 Qxf6 Bxf6 30 Re6. Black is slightly better, but there is no reason why White with sound play should not draw. But, instead, White plays the "active":

29 h4?   Qxg5
30 hxg5   Be5!

Suddenly it becomes clear what White's "attacking" 29th move has brought: his g5 pawn is indefensible and after losing it, not only White will be a pawn down but, moreover, his king position will be seriously weakened.

31 Kh2   Rf7
32 Re6

White's weak pawns are lost also in the rook + pawn endgame after 32 Rxe5 dxe5 33 d6 Kf8 34 Bxf7 Kxf7.

32 . . .   Rg7
33 f3   Rxg5
34 Rh6   Rb7
35 Re1   Rbg7
36 Re2   Rg3

37 Ra2   R7g6
38 Rh5   Bd4

and in this hopeless position White overstepped the time limit and lost.

The mutual opportunities for exchanging queens on your terms are well illustrated from Diagram 89,

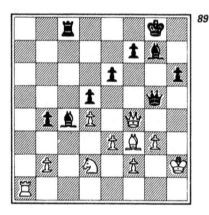

89

O. Romanishin – V. Hort, Dortmund 1982, after White's 28th move. With Black to move, he can exchange on *his* terms with the straightforward 28 . . . Qxf4. After 29 gxf4 Bd3! 30 Bd1 Bf8 (analysis by Hort after the game) Black has a slight but clear advantage: his rook + bishops stand well and the h-pawn is passed. White, for his part, has no compensation for his doubled f-pawns. Yet in the game Black, wanting more, played:

28 . . .   e5?!

attacking the queen and opening the diagonal of the king's bishop. Black looks forward to 29 Qxg5?! hxg5 when his kingside pawn formation is improved and his king's bishop will be menacing the b-pawn. However, White crosses up these plans with . . .

29 Qg4!   Qxg4

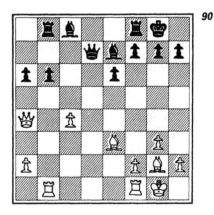

The attack on the rook must of course be attended to. The active 29 . . . f5?! exposes the king to a bishop check on d5 and thus White has 30 Qxg5 hxg5 31 dxe5 Bxe5 32 Rc1!. White threatens both 33 b3 and 33 Bxd5 and 32 . . . Bxb2? also is met by 33 Bxd5+!

30 Bxg4   Re8

Black must give up the c-file (30 . . . Rc7? 31 Ra8+ Kh7?? 32 Bf5 mate) and thus the game simplifies to static equality.

31 dxe5
Draw

After 31 . . . Bxe5 32 Ra4 Bxb2 White can play both 33 Rxb4 Bc3 34 Rxc4 dxc4 35 Nxc4 and 33 Nxc4 dxc4 34 Rxb4 c3 35 Rc4 to hold the draw.

The previous two examples were fairly basic. A more sophisticated example occurs from Diagram 90, I. Ivanov – V. Frias, Los Angeles 1982, after Black's 17th move. (The moves up to then were 1 d4 Nf6 2 Nf3 e6 3 c4 c5 4 g3 cxd4 5 Nxd4 Bb4+ 6 Bd2 Be7 7 Bg2 Nc6 8 e3 Nxd4?! 9 exd4 0-0 10 Nc3 d5 11 cxd5 Nxd5?! 12 0-0 Nxc3 13 bxc3 Rb8 14 Rb1 b6?! 15 Qa4! a6 16 c4! Qxd4 17 Be3 Qd7.) White can, of course, win back the sacrificed pawn with 18 Qxd7 Bxd7 19 Rxb6 or 19 Bxb6, but since Black's development has become smoothly completed, his disadvantage is small. Note also that 19 Rfd1?! just wastes time since Black has 19 . . . Ba4 in response. Instead, Ivanov spies a very creative way of exchanging queens while retaining a major positional advantage:

18 Qc6!!   Qxc6

This does not work out satisfactorily. But neither is 18 . . . b5 any better because of 19 Bf4! Qxc6

(19 . . . Rb7 just loses time after 20 Rfd1!) 20 Bxc6 Rb6 21 axb5 and White will have a very powerful passed a-pawn.

19	Bxc6	Bb7
20	Rxb6	Bxc6
21	Rxc6	Rfc8
22	Rxa6	Rxc4
23	Rd1	

The combination of active white pieces and the passed a-pawn add up to a very superior endgame and White realizes his advantage impressively.

23	. . .	Rbc8
24	Ra7!	Bc5
25	Rad7!	f5
26	Rd8+	Rxd8

27	Rxd8+	Bf8
28	a4!	

The exchange of rooks has removed a defender and with the help of tactics (28 . . . Rxa4? 29 Bc5) the a-pawn is mobilized. Passed pawns must be pushed!

28	. . .	Kf7
29	a5	Be7
30	Ra8	Bf6
31	a6	Bd4
32	a7!	Bxe3
33	Rf8+	Kxf8
34	a8=Q+	Kf7
35	fxe3	h5
36	Qh8	g6
37	Kf2	Re4
38	Qh7+	Kf6
39	Qg8	

Black resigns

17

Exchanging Queens as a Defense Mechanism

There is hardly a position which does not *appear* safer with queens off. Still, queens should only then be exchanged if it is objectively in our interest to do so. This chapter will consider defensive techniques. The two important defensive situations where exchanging queens is in order are consolidation and prevention of counterplay. It is often just as important to threaten to exchange queens as it is to achieve this. If the exchange is very unpleasant to your opponent, he will try to avoid it and often enough at high cost. Thus by threatening to exchange you can often get your opponent to start digging his own grave.

The concept of "preventing counterplay" is generally well understood. Yet the meaning of "consolidation" is not clear to many players and therefore I shall start with this.

1. Consolidation

I shall use the help of the dictionary to make the meaning clearer. *Webster's New Collegiate Dictionary* lists three meanings of which the following one applies to us: to consolidate means to make firm or secure. In chess terms this means that we want to make secure our position. What I am talking about is well illustrated from Diagram 91, Le Zunian – R. Her-

(see following diagram)

nandez, Lucerne Olympiad 1982, after Black's 46th move. White is up a pawn, yet Black has genuine attacking chances because of his active queen and the doubled rooks pressuring White's g-pawn. Therefore White wants to consolidate ("make secure his position"):

47 Qb6!

91

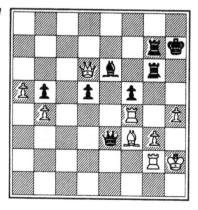

This is considerably more effective than 47 Re2 Qa7! since 48 Rxe6?? loses after 48 . . . Qf2+ 49 Kh1 Qxg3! and otherwise Black is again menacing the g-pawn.

47 . . .   Qe1

The endgame after 47 . . . Qxb6 48 axb6 (if 48 . . . Rb7, 49 Rd2) is lost since White will wind up at least a pawn ahead and with all of Black's pawns vulnerable to White's bishop.

48 Qg1!	Qe5
49 Qd4!	Qe1?

Obviously both retreating and exchanging are unpleasant. Therefore Black "decides" to dig his own grave.

50 Rg1!
Black resigns

Notice how White's powerfully centralized queen, in coordination with the rest of the pieces, has cut off all of the black queen's retreat squares.

The most common need for consolidation comes as a result of having won material somewhere on the board. This invariably costs a tempo or two and it is imperative that the opponent not be given the time to make effective use of this. A model case is demonstrated from Diagram 92, O. Romanishin – G. Kasparov, USSR 1982, after

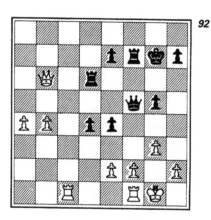

92

Black's 28th move. White's queen has captured pawns on Black's queenside to give White a one pawn advantage and connected passed pawns on the queenside. In the meanwhile Black has created a menacing center and attacking chances against White's king. White's objective must be to consolidate his position sufficiently so that the passed pawns can become the decisive element. White's play is crystal clear:

29 Qc5!	Rd5
30 Qc8!	Qe5
31 Rc5!	

Notice how White's threat to exchange queens has allowed him to consolidate sufficiently so that he can now achieve a rook exchange. This yields further consolidation and the exchange of a defender also makes it easier for White to mobilize his passed pawns.

31 . . .	e6
32 a5!	e3
33 f4!	gxf4
34 Rxf4	Rxf4
35 gxf4	Qf5

The effectively placed combination of White's queen and rook win after 35 . . . Qxf4 36 Rc7+ Kf6 37 Qh8+. Yet now White consolidates his advantage into a winning queen + pawn ending.

36 Rxd5!	Qxd5
37 Qc7+	Kg6
38 Qc2+	Kf6
39 a6!	Qa8
40 Qc4	Qe4
41 Qc5	Qb1+

Obviously 41 . . . Qxf4 loses to 42 Qf8+. Nor is there hope in 41 . . . Kf7 42 a7 d3 (if 42 . . . Qxf4, 43 Qh5+ Kg7 44 Qf3!) 43 Qh5+ Kg7 44 exd3 e2 45 dxe4.

42 Kg2	Qd1
43 Qg5+	Kf7
44 Qh5+	Kg7
45 a7	
Black resigns

In the next example, Diagram 93, L. Kavalek – J. Timman, Wijk aan Zee 1982, after Black's 20th

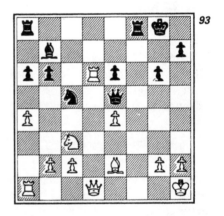

move, we see the actual exchange of queens as part of the consolidation operation. White is up a pawn as a result of capturing a vulnerable d-pawn on d6. The usual reaction has also taken place: Black's pieces have been activated, Black's queen has a powerful post on e5 and

Black's pieces menace the e-pawn directly and after its capture, White's kingside will be under pressure. Very risky for White now is, for example, 21 Rxb6?! because of 21 . . . Nxe4! 22 Nxe4 Bxe4. The correct strategy is consolidation.

21 Qd4!   Qxd4

Leaving White's queen powerfully placed on d4 is even less attractive, e.g. 21 . . . Qf4 22 Kg1!, with White threatening 23 Rxb6 as well as further consolidation by 23 Rf1.

| 22 | Rxd4 | e5 |
| 23 | Rd6! | b5!? |

Worse is 23 . . . Nxe4?! 24 Bc4+ Kh8 25 Rxb6 Nxc3 26 Rxb7 with both a material and positional advantage for White.

24 Rb6!   Bxe4

24 . . . bxa4? 25 Nxa4 Nxa4 26 Rxa4 leaves White with a sound extra pawn.

| 25 | Nxe4 | Nxe4 |
| 26 | Kg1! | Rfb8! |

Black has been putting up the best defense, but with 27 Rc6! (suggested by Kavalek after the game) White would retain a clear advantage as a result of the active rooks, superior minor piece and weak black pawns. For instance, 27 . . . Rc8 is unsatisfactory because of 28 axb5 axb5 29 Rxc8+! Rxc8 30 Bxb5 Rxc2? 31 Bd3. As played, White lacks sufficient attacking power to take advantage of Black's weaknesses on b5 and e5.

27	Rxb8+?	Rxb8
28	axb5	axb5
29	Re1	Nd6
30	Bf3	Rc8
31	c3	Rc5
32	b4	Rxc3
33	Rxe5	Kf8
34	Be2	
	Draw	

2. Prevention of counterplay

It is hardly a secret that the queen is a very powerful piece. Less recognized is the fact that the power of the queen is significantly enhanced if it gets help. This help can come from the king, from other pieces or from pawns. Conversely, very often an attack loses all of its punch if the attacking queen can be exchanged off. Therefore, if the presence of the enemy queen prevents you from doing what you would like to, work to exchange it off. This then will allow you to do your own thing.

A good example to start this discussion is Diagram 94, W. Uhlmann – A Adorjan, Budapest 1982, after White's 35th move. For

94

the Exchange, White has two pawns and thus even a slight material advantage. However, overall the situation is favorable to Black because of the following factors: White's bishop is passive whereas Black's is active, White's queenside pawns and e-pawn are vulnerable, White's rook is passive, whereas Black's rooks are well placed. Yet there is one thing that prevents Black from exploiting his strengths: his weakened king position. The dark squares (h6, g7, f6) are chronically weak and the movement of the h-pawn to h4 has weakened g6. These weaknesses show up dramatically if Black plays 38 . . . Qxb4?, because 39 Nxg6! fxg6 (forced) 40 Qxg6+ leads to perpetual check.

With the above discussion in mind, Black's correct course becomes clear:

35 . . .	Qd4!
36 Qxd4	

Forced, since otherwise the rook hangs.

36 . . .	Rxd4
37 Rc1	Rc8!

The wisdom behind Black's 35th move is already obvious: the king is absolutely secure and Black's remaining three pieces are so active that he gains a pawn immediately.

38 Bf1	Bxe4
39 a3	a5
40 Ng2	f5!

Black plays actively to keep his pieces at maximum effectiveness while denying White's knight a good defensive location on e3, as after 40 . . . g5 41 Ne3. I believe that the latter course also would in the long run be sufficient for a black win.

41 Nxh4	g5!
42 Ng2	f4!
43 bxa5	

Because Black's pieces are just so much better placed than White's, White has no satisfactory defense.

Adorjan provides the following two examples: 43 Ne1 Rcd8; 43 h4 axb4 44 axb4 gxh4 45 Nxf4 Bd5! 46 Nxd5 exd5!.

43 . . .	**Rc5**
44 h4	**Rxa5**
45 c5	**Bc6**
46 hxg5	**Rxa3**
47 Bc4	**Re4**
48 Ne1	**f3!**

Ensuring that Black's active position will lead to the capture of the g-pawns, with resulting decisive material and positional superiority. Less clear is the tactical 48 . . . Rxc4?! because after 49 Rxc4 Ra1 50 Rxf4 Rxe1+ 51 Kh2, White will play Rf6 followed by f4 and f5. White then has counterplay and excellent chances to gain a draw by exchanging off Black's last pawn.

49 Kh2	**Kg7**
50 Bf1	**Rxg4**
51 Bh3	**Rxg5**
52 Rc4	**Ra2**
53 Rc2	**Ra8!**
54 Rc3	**Rf8**
55 Rd3	

The bishop is lost after 55 Bxe6? Rh8+ 56 Bh3 Rgh5. Even after the text, White's days are numbered.

55 . . .	**Rf6!**
56 Rd6	**e5**
57 Nc2	**e4**

58 Nd4	**Rxc5!**
59 Ne6+	**Kf7**
60 Kg3	**Ke7**
White resigns	

An even clearer example of the strategy of exchanging queens to prevent counterplay is demonstrated from Diagram 95, L. Ljubojevic – J. Timman, Bugojno 1982,

95

after Black's 32nd move. White's great strengths are the connected passed pawns on the queenside. Note how poorly placed Black's minor pieces are for coping with them. But Black's queen and three minor pieces are in a position to get at White's king. It is true that White seems to be in no concrete danger. But anything can happen in the future—thus why take any chances at all? Therefore White—a grandmaster who is never afraid of the most hair-raising complications—

plays to prevent any *potential* black counterplay:

33 Qc3!   Qxc3

Inherently hopeless, yet neither is there hope after 33 . . . Qd6 34 Rc8+ Nf8 (or 34 . . . Nd8 35 Qc7) 35 Qc5!.,

34	Rxc3	Nf6
35	f3	g4
36	e5!	Nd5
37	Rc8+	Kg7
38	Bb3	Ne7
39	Bxe6	fxe6
40	Rc7	Kf8
41	f4	Nf5
42	Rc3	h5

The open position of White's king would be quite a problem with queens on. Yet here the king is absolutely safe and the Q-side pawns win in a walk.

43	a4	h4
44	a5	

Black resigns

The a-pawn queens after 44 . . . hxg3 45 a6 Nd4 46 Rxg3! Ne2+ 47 Kh2 Nxg3 48 Kxg3.

If you are ahead in material, but the realization of your plan is a problem because of potential counterplay, do consider giving back the excess material (or part of it) so as to kill any or all the counterplay.

Still, giving back material should never be done lightly, but only after very serious consideration. An excellent example of when such a decision is correct is shown from Diagram 96, Cunningham – R. Henley, USA 1982, after White's 25th move. Black is a pawn up.

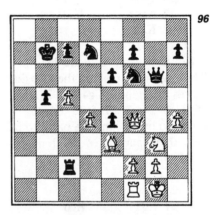

96

However, it is easy enough to see that Black's major trump is the passed b-pawn which he would like to advance and promote. But such an advance denudes Black's king position and White's active queen and rook are well placed to exploit this. Theoretically speaking, Black should with perfect play be able to execute the plan of advancing the b-pawn. Yet in a real game, a moment of carelessness is always possible. Moreover, note that Black's queen is not at all able to help directly with the pawn's advance. Based on such considerations, grandmaster Henley fashions the plan of exchanging queens at the cost of the extra pawn so that he can work on exploiting his strength – the passed b-pawn – while preventing counterplay:

25 . . .	Nd5!
26 Qxe4	Qxe4
27 Nxe4	f6!
28 Kh2	

White tries to activate his king. The attempt to just use the kingside pawns also fails: 28 g4 Kc6 29 g5 f5 30 Ng3 Nxe3 31 fxe3 b4 to be followed by pushing the pawn to b2 and then playing . . . Rc1 (Cunningham).

28 . . .	b4!
29 Kg3	Kc6
30 Rb1	Kb5!

It now is clear that Black's one pawn investment on move 25 has been well worth it: the King's knight has a powerful, unassailable location on d5, Black has the active rook, the b-pawn is ready to move and Black's king, rather than being in danger, has instead become a powerful attacker. White is lost strategically and has no chances for counterplay—the worst kind of situation to find yourself in.

| 31 Kf3 | Nb8! |
| 32 g4 | Nc6 |

| 33 g5 | fxg5! |
| 34 hxg5 | |

Or 34 Nxg5 e5! 35 dxe5 Nxe5+ 36 Kg3 h5! with a won position for Black (Henley).

34 . . .	Kc4!
35 Nf6	Nc3
36 Rh1	b3
37 Nxh7	Ne7!
38 Nf8	Kd5
39 g6	b2
40 Bg5	Nf5
White resigns	

Black's b-pawn will cost White a whole rook.

I can guarantee that bad things will happen to those who only think of themselves. Look at Diagram 97 which arose in G. Sax – A. Martin, Hastings 1983/84, after Black's 27th move. White has won a pawn and has a clear advantage by virtue of

97

having a sound 3 P vs. 1 P majority on the queenside. However, White's king position is very weak on the light squares: f3, h3 and in particular g2. In an endgame White would have no problems, but with queens on extreme care is required. Everyone who has carefully gone over the previous three examples would now play 28 Qc5!. White thereby removes his queen from being attacked, does so with a gain of time by threatening to exchange queens, while at the same time preventing Black's threat. Whether Black exchanges queens or plays it to d7 or e6, White keeps his advantage. Yet White, concerned only with himself plays:

28 Qh5??

By threatening the h-pawn he thinks that he is gaining time, yet Black's counterplay comes first!

28 . . .	Qc6!!
29 Qxh7+	

The defensive 29 f3 allows 29 . . . Rxe3.

29 . . .	Kf8
30 Qh8+	

This is the main line. In the game White played the desperate 30 Bc5+ and resigned after 30 . . . Qxc5 31 Kg1 (31 Qh8+ Ke7 32 Re4+ Kd6!) 31 . . . Re1 32 Qh8+ Ke7 33 Rd4 Bh3+, in view of the mating combination 34 Kh2 Rh1+!! 35 Kxh1 Qc6+ 36 Kh2 Qg2 mate.

30 . . .	Ke7
31 Bg5+	Kd7
32 Rd4+	Kc8
33 Rd8+	Kc7!
Black wins	

18

Exchanging Queens as an Offensive Mechanism

The queen is not only very powerful in the attack, but also is a marvelous defender. Just by itself the queen can cover various vulnerable points. (Moreover, at any moment it can change its spots and become an attacker.) Therefore, quite often the enemy queen must be exchanged off so that you can make progress. This was already discussed in Chapter 5 as far as endgames are concerned. The even more important application is in the transition from the middlegame to the endgame and this is presented in the first part of this chapter.

Since the queen is such a powerful piece you do want to have it active. Sometimes this can be achieved by offering to exchange it. If your opponent cannot afford to exchange on the terms that you offer—presto, your queen has been activated! This technique is discussed in the second part of this chapter.

1. Removing the key defender

As mentioned above, very often the key defender is the queen. If you can remove it by an exchange, then the enemy position becomes much more vulnerable. Sometimes it simply collapses. This can even occur early in the game. Our first position, Diagram 98, L. Vogt – L. Barczay, Trnava 1982 is after Black's 12th move. (The game

98

score up to here is: 1 Nf3 Nf6 2 c4 g6 3 Nc3 Bg7 4 e4 d6 5 d4 0-0 6 Be2 e5 7 0-0 exd4?! 8 Nxd4 Re8 9 f3 c6 10 Kh1! d5? 11 cxd5 cxd5 12 Bg5! dxe4.) Black has embarked on a dubious center liquidating maneuver, while neglecting his queenside development. This game, with the upcoming shot, put an end to Black's opening variation:

13 Ndb5!!

Black, no doubt, realized that he is behind in development in the diagrammed position. But he counted on completing it well enough. Then the lack of a pawn center will lead to approximate equality.

White's development is complete and he sees that after Black's best defender — the queen — is removed, that Black will be unable to cope with the weaknesses on c7, d6, along the f-file and the curse of the undeveloped queenside.

13 ...   **Qxd1**

There is nothing more satisfactory. White threatened 14 Qxd8 Rxd8 15 Nc7; 13 ... Nc6 (or ... Na6) 14 Qxd8 Rxd8 15 fxe4 makes the king's knight indefensible.

14 Raxd1   **Na6**
15 fxe4!

Without his queen, Black's position is too porous against White's active pieces. Immediately catastrophic is 15 ... Nxe4? 16 Nxe4 Rxe4 17 Rd8+ Bf8 18 Bh6.

15 ...   **Nh5**
16 Nd6   **Bxc3**

Or 16 ... Re5 17 Nxf7; or 16 ... Rf8 17 g4 h6 18 Be7.

17 Nxe8
Black resigns

After 17. . . Bxb2 18 Rd8 Black is defenseless.

Of course, the effect need not be that drastic to justify an early queen exchange. This is also quite the correct approach from Diagram 99, G. Timoshchenko – R. Holmov, USSR 1982, after Black's 12th move. (The game score up to here is: 1 d4 Nf6 2 c4 e6 3 g3 d5 4 Nf3

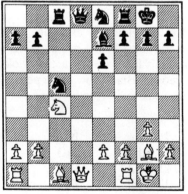

99

dxc4 5 Bg2 c5 6 0-0 Nbd7 7 Na3 cxd4 8 Nxc4 Be7?! 9 Nxd4 0-0 10 Nb5! Nc5 11 Nbd6 Ne8 12 Nxc8 Rxc8.) Although the pawn formation is symmetrical and Black has no permanent weaknesses, White's advantage is both clear and comfortable. Already White's king's bishop applies very strong pressure against Black's queenside. Thanks to having the bishop pair, White can anticipate that after developing his queen's bishop, both of White's bishops will be raking Black's queenside. If Black's best defender—the queen—is not on the board, White's pressure will be even stronger. Therefore:

13 Qxd8!	Rxd8
14 Be3	b6
15 Ne5	Bf6
16 Nc6	Rd7
17 Rad1!	Bxb2
18 Rxd7	Nxd7
19 Nxa7	

By the judicious exchange of a pair of rooks, White has made sure that he is left with the active rook. Moreover, Black now has a permanent weakness— the b6 pawn.

19 . . .	Nef6
20 Rb1	Ba3
21 Rb3	Bd6
22 Bc6!	Bb8?

Black's position cannot afford this passive bishop placement. Timoshchenko suggests 22 . . . Bc7 as Black's only defense with best play then being 23 Nb5 Bd8 24 Nc3! and a continuing clear advantage for White.

| 23 Bxd7! | Nxd7 |

After 23 . . . Bxa7 24 Bc6! Rb8 (otherwise 25 Bxb6) 25 Ra3! Black's bishop is lost.

| 24 Nc6 | Bc7 |
| 25 Ra3! | |

The point of White's bishop exchange on move 23 is now clear: White's active pieces (all three!) easily outpoint Black's awkward passive forces.

25 . . .	Nf6
26 Ra7	Nd5
27 Bd4	Bd8?

Loses instantly. But even in case of the correct 27 . . . f5 28 Ne7+ Nxe7 29 Rxc7 Re8, after 30 Rb7!, followed by 31 Bxb6, White's win is assured.

28 e4	Nf6
29 Ra8	
Black resigns	

The attacked bishop cannot move, since 29 . . . Bc7 allows 30

Ne7+. What an easy time White had in the endgame in taking over Black's queenside!

Now let us move to full-fledged middlegame positions, i.e. those where both sides have completed their initial development. An excellent example is the play from Diagram 100, G. Sax – M. Quinteros, Moscow Interzonal 1982, after Black's 18th move. Black has many

chronic weaknesses on the queenside: the a5, b7 and d6 pawns, as well as the b5 and b6 squares. Yet Black's queen stands guard over everything. Therefore White's approach should by now be clear:

19 Qc4!	Qxc4
20 Bxc4	Rc8
21 Bb5!	

According to Sax, a good alternative is 21 Nxa5 Bd8 22 Nxb7 Rxc4

23 Nxd6. Yet to my mind it is quite correct to avoid any kind of complication.

21 ...	Bd8
22 g4	Nfd7
23 Nd2	Bb6
24 Bg5!	

White here gives a marvelous example of exchanging only on his terms. If instead 24 Bxb6?! Nxb6, then Black's knight controls c4 and the king's rook is able to defend the d-pawn after 25 Ne4. Black is then safe enough.

24 ...	Bd8

This is not satisfactory, but then again, nothing is. White had the triple threats of Be7, Nc4 and Ne4. If 24 ... f6 25 Bh4 g5, then 26 Be1 followed by 27 Nc4 leads to problems with the a-pawn, whereas 24 ... Rc5 25 Bxd7 Nxd7 26 Ne4 costs Black the d-pawn.

25 Bxd8!	Rfxd8
26 Nc4	Rc7
27 Nxd6	

White, having a choice, prefers the d-pawn since now his d-pawn becomes a powerful passed pawn.

27 ...	Nf6
28 Nf5!	Rc5

The d-pawn is taboo, as 28 . . . Nxd5? 29 c4 pins the knight, as does 28 . . . Rxd5? 29 Rxd5 Nxd5 30 Rd1 (30 . . . Rc5 31 Rxd5!).

| 29 c4 | Na6 |

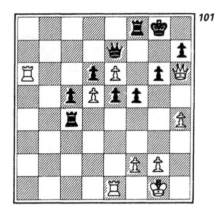

Since 29 . . . Nxd5? is refuted by 30 Ne7+, Black remains a pawn down in a bad position. Mutual time pressure is the explanation for Black's continuing to play until move 40.

30	Rhe1	Nc7
31	b4	axb4
32	axb4	Rxb5
33	cxb5	Nxb5
34	Kb2	g6
35	Nh6+	Kg7
36	g5	Nd7
37	Ng4	Re8
38	d6	Re6
39	Nxe5!	Nxe5
40	d7	
Black resigns		

Even if the middlegame position looks complicated, always have the queen exchange strategy in your offensive "bag of tricks". A most appropriate illustration of this occurs from Diagram 101, A. Adorjan – T. Horvath, 1984 Hungarian Championship, after Black's 24th move. White has sacrificed a pawn to obtain a promising position: good attacking chances against

Black's king, a powerful protected passed pawn on e6, and a vulnerable Black d-pawn, the capture of which would give White connected passed pawns. The glue that holds the black position together is most certainly his Queen, so:

| 25 Qg5! | Qxg5 |

The inherent vulnerability of Black's position is shown up dramatically with the queens off. Yet attempts to keep the queen on are also drastically refuted: (a) 25 . . . Rf6 26 Ra7! Qxa7 27 Qxf6 with Black helpless against the coming e-pawn advance, (b) 25 . . . Qc7 26 Rc6! Qb8 (26 . . . Qa5 27 Rf1 is just an insignificant interlude) 27 Qe7 etc.

| 26 hxg5 | Rd8 |
| 27 Rea1! | Rb4 |

Hoping to defend against 28 Ra8 by 28 . . . Rbb8, but White has an immediate *coup de grace*. Instead, 27 . . . Kf8 would lose more prosaically after 28 Ra7 etc.

28 Rxd6!
Black resigns

White's pawn queens after 28 . . . Rxd6 29 Ra8+ Kg7 30 e7 and Black's rook checks fall short of perpetual.

2. Activating your queen

By offering to exchange queens you can achieve other offensive goals, if your opponent cannot afford to exchange on the terms that you offer. The most important such goal is to activate your queen. This is excellently demonstrated from Diagram 102, A. Matanovic –

R. Henley, Indonesia 1982, after White's 20th move. Black's very active piece placement (both rooks, both knights and the bishop are excellently placed) more than compensate the isolated d-pawn. Moreover, many of White's pieces have awkward and passive locations. Black already has the advantage. If the modest location of his queen could be improved, his advantage would increase. Therefore:

20 . . .   Qc4!
21 Nc1

Understandably, White wants the queens to be exchanged on his terms, but, of course, Black is not about to oblige. Instead, 21 Qxc4?! dxc4 rids Black of his isolated pawn, while making White's b-pawn more vulnerable and creating a new weakness on d3. The retreat, 21 Qc2, is also unattractive because after 21 . . . b4 White will be left with a vulnerable pawn on c3. Yet the text move "undevelops" a piece and gives Black the opportunity to even further activitate *his* pieces.

21 . . .	Ng5!
22 Rd1	Nc5!
23 Bxc5	Nxf3+
24 Qxf3	Bxc5
25 Nb3	Bb6
26 Rd2	Re4!

The coming doubling of rooks on the e-file will further increase Black's pressure and advantage. Note how powerfully Black's queen is placed on her unassailable location.

27	Rf1	Rde8
28	Rdd1	Re2!
29	Rxd5	Rxb2
30	Rd6	Bc7!
31	Rd7	

The active location of Black's queen prevents 31 Rxa6? because of 31 . . . Qxf1+! 32 Kxf1 Rb1+ with mate to follow.

| 31 | . . . | Rxa2! |
| 32 | Nd2 | Qf4! |

Black's approach to winning the game is picture perfect. First, the active location of his pieces is utilized to win an important pawn. Now the queens are exchanged to minimize any chances for counterplay. Black's handling of the coming ending is sound enough and I will give the moves for the record only, without further comments.

33	g3	Qxf3
34	Nxf3	Bd8
35	Rd6	Be7
36	Rc6	Bf8
37	c4	bxc4
38	Rxc4	Ree2
39	Nd4	Red2

40	Nb3	Rdb2
41	Nc5	a5
42	Nd7	Bd6
43	Nf6+	Kf8
44	Nxh7+	Kg7
45	Ng5	Bxg3!
46	Ne4	Be5
47	Rd1	Rc2
48	Rxc2	Rxc2
49	Rd7	a4
50	Ra7	Ra2
51	Ng5	Kf6
52	h4	Bd4
53	Rxf7+	Ke5
54	Nf3+	Ke6
55	Ng5+	Kd5
56	Rd7+	Kc4
57	Rc7+	Kb5
58	Ne4	Re2!
59	Nc3+	Bxc3
60	Rxc3	Re4!
61	Rg3	Rxh4
62	Rxg6	a3
63	Rg5+	Kb4
64	Re5	a2
65	Re1	Kc3
66	Kg2	Ra4!
67	Ra1	Kb2
68	Rxa2+	Kxa2
69	Kg3	Kb3
White resigns		

In our next example, Diagram 103, A. Bachtiar – R. Henley, Indonesia, 1982, after White's 24th move, we see an enhancement of

(see following diagram)

103

the technique of activating the queen by offering to have it exchanged. Not only does Black activate his queen thus, but this serves as the beginning of the campaign to deactivate White's queen. In the diagrammed position Black has a number of clear advantages: active doubled rooks, the superior bishop, and a sound queenside pawn formation whereas White's pawns are split there. However, the out-of-action position of Black's queen makes it difficult to make progress. Therefore:

24 . . .   Qb4!
25 Rf3?!

There are no reasons why White's attempt at an attack should be successful. Yet the endgame prospects after 25 Qxb4 Bxb4 26 Bd6 Bxd6 27 Rxd6 Rc8 28 Rc1 Rc3!

also are dim. Perhaps the best try is to play 25 Rfd1 and to hope.

25 . . .   a5!
26 c3

If now 26 Qxb4, Black's last move has enabled the recapture with the a-pawn, 26 . . . axb4, followed by . . . Ra8 and the inevitable capture of White's a-pawn.

After White's text move, Black is not about to exchange, since 26 . . . Qxb3?! 27 axb3 straightens out White's pawns and greatly increases his drawing chances. Instead, Black further activates its queen.

26 . . .   Qe4!
27 Rd1   a4!
28 Qb2

This modest queen location allows Black's queen to decisively tower over its rival. Yet there are no satisfactory moves. Henley provides the following proof: 28 Qb5 Qc2!; 28 Qd5 Qxd5 29 Rxd5 Re2 30 Bd6 Rxf2! 31 Rxf2 Re1+; 28 Qb1 Qxb1 29 Rxb1 Re1+ 30 Rxe1 Rxe1+ 31 Kh2 Ra1.

28 . . .   Qc4!
29 Rfd3   Re1+
30 Kh2   R1e2
31 R3d2   h5!

With White tied up in knots, this direct attack scores quickly.

32 Rxe2	Rxe2
33 Rd8+	

Or 33 Rd2 Re1! followed by . . . Qf1 (Henley).

33 . . .	Kh7
34 Qb1+	g6
35 h4	Bxf2
36 Bxf2	Qc7+

White resigns

19

Playing the Balanced Middlegame: When Should the Queens be Exchanged

The balanced middlegame is usually the natural result of a game well played by both sides. Black has neutralized White's first move advantage and now chances are equal. If the opening has been of a solid type, then it is likely that each side has a healthy position with hardly a weakness. It should be of no surprise that in such a situation it does not matter whether the queens are exchanged or not. If we sharpen the opening variation, the possibilities for dynamic play will increase of course, but still each side will have a good position and the exchange of queens should not disturb this. Even if we have a very complicated position—as long as both sides have played perfectly—whether or not we exchange queens generally does not affect the objective evaluation of the position.

Look at Diagram 104, Zelensky – Praslov, USSR Correspondence

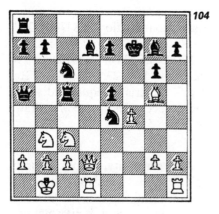

104

1981, after Black's 17th move (the game score: 1 e4 c5 2 Nf3 d6 3 d4 cxd4 4 Nxd4 Nf6 5 Nc3 g6 6 Be3 Bg7 7 f3 Nc6 8 Qd2 0-0 9 Bc4 Qa5 10 Bb3 Bd7 11 0-0-0 Rfc8 12 Kb1 Ne5 13 Bg5 Rc5 14 f4 Nc6 15 e5 dxe5 16 Bxf7+ Kxf7 17 Nb3 Ne4!). White has started a very dangerous attack, yet Black demonstrates that with perfect defense the position remains in balance—whether White exchanges queens or not. Praslov provides the following analysis as proof:

(1) *White keeps queens on:* 18 Qxd7 Nxc3+ 19 bxc3 Rb5 20 f5 (20 fxe5 Nxe5! with = chances) 20 . . . gxf5 21 Qxf5+ Kg8 22 Rd3 e4 23 Qe6+ Kh8 24 Rg3 (24 Rh3? is refuted by 24 . . . Rxb3+! followed by 25 . . . Qxg5) 24 . . . Qd8 25 Qxe4 a5! with equal chances.

(2) *White exchanges queens* (game continuation): 18 Nxe4 Qxd2 19 Rxd2 Rc4 20 Rxd7 Rxe4 21 Rf1 (21 Rxb7 h6 22 Bh4 exf4) 21 . . . h6 22 fxe5+ Ke8 23 Bd2 b6! 24 Rc7 Nxe5. Material is equal and so are the chances. The game was drawn on move 51.

As a generality, from a theoretical (i.e. chess) standpoint, it usually is immaterial whether we exchange queens or not. Still, it may matter a great deal for either practical or psychological reasons.

Do not exchange queens if:

(1) You are playing for a win and your opponent is in time pressure.

(2) You are playing for a win— period.

(3) You generally feel more confident in positions with queens on.

Exchange queens if:

(1) You are playing for a draw.

(2) Only you are in time pressure.

(3) You are much more comfortable with queens off.

(4) Your opponent is weak in the endgame.

The times when it will matter for chess reasons whether the queens are exchanged or not will be in a clear minority — in the 25 – 30% range. Yet this is frequently enough to require a knowledge of the type of situations which are the exceptions.

1. Exchanging your queen is the correct plan

In general you want to exchange queens, if the enemy queen applies pressure on your position. A perfect example is shown in Diagram 105, U. Andersson – A. Miles,

(see following diagram)

London 1984, after White's 21st move. White's rooks have complete

105

White could make no progress and the game was called a draw after:

24	Bf3	Kg7
25	Kg2	f5!?
26	d4	Rc4
27	b3	Rc3!
28	R7e3	Rc2
29	R1e2	Rc1
30	Re1	Rc2
31	R1e2	Rc1
32	Re1	
Draw		

control of the important open e-file and his queen has a domineering location on d4. Such a combination can very easily lead to excellent middle-game prospects for White. Black's response is very instructive:

21	...	Qf6!!
22	Qxf6	gxf6
23	Re7	Bc8!

Inferior is 23 . . . Rd8?! 24 Bf3! and White threatens 25 Bh5. After the text move, the essence of the position is quite different from that of our starting point. It is an endgame and to win White must be able to capture a pawn or two. Even though Black's pawn formation looks ugly, White cannot get at Black's pawns. Therefore this endgame is readily defensible for Black. Of course, White is handicapped because his bishop is rather impotent. In the further course

Of course, it does not necessarily have to be the queen position that is the critical element in determining who is the one applying pressure. Consider Diagram 106, J. Timman – V. Smyslov, Tilburg 1982, after Black's 36th move. The queen positions are about equal, yet it is not difficult to see that the combination of Black's rook, a-pawn, bishop pair and aided by the presence of

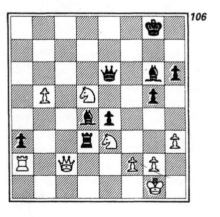

106

the queen, exerts uncomfortable pressure against White's position. Moreover, the path forward of White's b-pawn is stymied. White takes care of all of these problems with:

37 Qc6!   Qxc6
38 bxc6

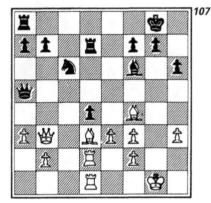

The exchange of the queens has both reduced Black's attacking chances as well as removed an effective defender. Suddenly Black has to worry about White's passed pawn and the chances are equal.

38 . . .   Bxe3
39 Nxe3

More complicated, yet also equal is the variation 39 c7 Bf5 40 Nxe3 Bc8 41 Rc2 Rd6 followed by 42 . . . Ra6 (Smyslov).

39 . . .   Rc3
40 c7   Rxc7
Draw

A natural way to squelch incipient attacks is to exchange off the strongest attacker—the queen. This is well demonstrated from Diagram 107, W. Browne – A. Karpov, Tilburg 1982, after Black's 19th move. Black has just played 19 . . . d4 and is now ready to swing his queen over to the kingside to menace White's king, made vulner-

able by the broken pawn cover. Clearly this must be prevented and White plays the only correct move:

20 Qb5!   Qxb5
21 Bxb5   Rad8

This resulting endgame is far from dead, yet the chances are dynamically equal.

22 Kf1   Rd5!
23 Bxc6   bxc6
24 e4   Rb5
25 e5

Or 25 b4 c5! with continuing equality.

25 . . .   Be7
26 Rxd4   Rxd4
27 Rxd4   Rxb2
28 Ra4!

Inferior is 28 Rd7? because after
28 . . . Bc5 29 Be3 Bxe3 30 fxe3
Rb3 White will lose a pawn.

28 . . .	Ra2
29 Rxa7	Bc5
30 Ra8+	Kh7
31 Bg3!	Rxa3
32 Rc8!	

White now has sufficient counterplay after 32 . . . Ra6 33 Rc7 Kg6
34 f4!. Therefore Karpov acquiesces to the draw.

32 . . .	Rxf3
33 Rxc6	Bd4
34 Rc4	Ba1
35 Re4!	
Draw	

2. Retaining your queen is the correct plan

You want to retain your queen if
it is the queen that provides the
necessary counterplay. Often there
is a fundamental problem in your
position—be it a weakened queenside, a weak pawn, weak square(s),
a temporarily misplaced piece, etc.
— yet your enemy can not concentrate on this because he has to
watch out for your prospects some-
place else. We call this dynamic
equality. If it is your queen that is

the basis for the play (or counterplay) that retains this dynamic
equality, it should be no surprise
that if you allow its exchange, your
"equality" disappears into inferiority.
A perfect illustration of this
occurs from Diagram 108, H.
Alford – E. Mednis, Florida 1982,

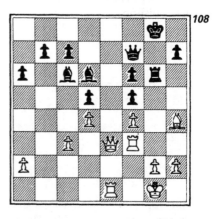

after White's 26th move. Black
is the exchange down for a pawn,
but has sufficient compensation:
White's bishop is impotent, White
has weak queenside pawns (in particular the a-pawn), Black controls
the centre squares. Yet Black cannot expect to throw all of his efforts
(i.e. pieces) against White's queenside, because then Black would be
short of defenders on the kingside.
White's queen and rooks could very
easily become menacing. Simply
stated: with queens on we have

dynamic equality. Let us now follow the instructive game course:

| 26 | . . . | Bb5 |

Of course, White's next could have been easily prevented by 26 . . . Bd7, but in fact I welcomed the queen exchange. In the meanwhile, I improve the position of my queen's bishop.

| 27 Qe6?! |

Any other reasonable move would have been better.

27	. . .	Qxe6
28	Rxe6	Kf7
29	Ree3	

The opposite color bishops and rook endgame after 29 Rxd6, though of course better for Black, should ultimately be drawn. But White never seems to realize that it is he who is worse in the endgame.

| 29 | . . . | Rg4! |

Black wants to force White to play h3 so that White can never activate a rook via that square.

30	Bg3	Bc4
31	Rf2	b5
32	h3	Rg8

33	Rb2	a5!
34	Rf3	Re8!
35	Bf2	a4!

Notice how free a hand Black has had on the queenside once the queens were off. White's position is close to critical and the only defense is 36 Be3!, preventing Black's next. After the game continuation White is lost.

36	g3?	Re2!
37	Rxe2	Bxe2
38	Re3	Bc4
39	Re1	Bxa2

White's vulnerable a-pawn has been lost. The only remaining question is whether Black can break through on the queenside.

40	Ra1	Bc4
41	Be3	a3
42	Bc1	a2
43	Bb2	h5
44	h4	c5!
45	Kf2	

After 45 dxc5 Bxc5+ White's king cannot reach the queenside. However, now Black gets connected passed pawns.

45	. . .	cxd4
46	cxd4	Ke6!
47	Re1+	Kd7
48	Re3	

If 48 Ke3, Black wins with 48 . . . Bb4!, followed by bringing his king to b3.

48 . . .	b4
49 Ke1	b3
50 Kd2	Bb4+!
51 Rc3	Ba3
52 Rxc4	dxc4
White resigns	

Part V

Winning Superior Middlegames

The culmination of successful opening play is the superior middlegame. Of all the world champions, Robert J. Fischer was an absolute whiz at obtaining this. Once *you* are in this situation you can feel very satisfied. Unfortunately, no game wins itself and you still have to both make the correct decisions and then execute them properly. The purpose of this part is to provide answers to both of the above needs.

Our goal in a superior middlegame is to choose that plan which will increase our overall prospects. In other words, either our winning chances should be increased, or the risk of losing decreased while retaining the same prospects of winning. Sometimes this will mean striving to exchange queens and sometimes keeping the queens on.

The kinds of situations where going directly for the middlegame kill is in order are considered in Chapter 20. Conversely, the times when middlegame complications should be avoided in favor of entering the endgame are discussed in Chapter 21. When we already have a material advantage in the middle game, this then is a natural situation to strive for the exchange of queens. This very important practical situation is explored fully in Chapter 22. There are also many types of positions where the positional advantage(s) are more readily realized in an endgame. These are presented in Chapter 23. Always remember that you only want to exchange queens when this does not decrease your winning prospects. A full description of when a queen exchange is undesirable appears in Chapter 24.

20

When to Go for the Middlegame Kill

A saying from long ago is "Strike while the iron is hot." You always want to keep this in mind when playing a superior middlegame. It surely is so much *safer* to gain a *quick* middlegame victory than to go through a laborious, though superior, endgame. The key guideline for evaluating whether to continue in the middlegame rather than simplifying into a superior endgame is: *stay in the middlegame if you have a massive near term superiority or your opponent has a massive immediate problem.*

An excellent, even though somewhat extreme, example of where the opponent has a massive immediate problem is shown in Diagram 109, J. Timman – T. Petrosian, Las Palmas Interzonal 1982, after White's 18th move. White is a pawn down and has no compensation for this. Black's "simplest" plan is 18 . . . Qxf2+ 19 Kxf2 e5, safeguarding the extra pawn. Theoretically speaking, this should be good enough to win in the long

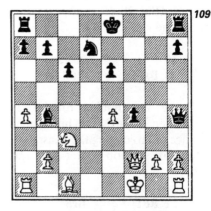

109

run. However, White would have some *practical* drawing chances, because his only remaining disadvantage is the missing pawn.

However, if we look at our starting position more closely, we see that White has also another major immediate problem: his king is precariously placed in the middle of the board and has already forfeited the right of castling. Therefore, even as careful a player as Petrosian sees that a continuing middlegame is the surest approach:

| 18 . . . | Qe7! |
| 19 e5?! | |

Black's f-pawn is an absolute pain in White's position and White therefore understandably wants to undermine and eliminate it. Otherwise after 19 . . . e5 White will not be able to breathe. Still, the punishment now is immediate. No better is 19 Bxf4?!, because then 19 . . . Rf8! 20 e5 transposes into the game continuation.

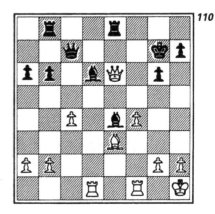

110

| 19 . . . | Nxe5 |
| 20 Bxf4 | Rf8! |

White was hoping for 20 . . . Nd3 when 21 Qd4! gives him a small chance of prolonging the resistance. There is no hope after the text move.

| 21 Rd1 | Bc5 |
| White resigns | |

He will be a piece down in an absolutely hopeless position (22 Qg3 Ng6; 22 Qd2 Nc4!).

A typical attacking position where the attacker has an immediate massive strength appears in Diagram 110, J. Nunn – J. Sunye, Wijk aan Zee 1982, after Black's 22nd move. White had earlier sacrificed a piece for two pawns. He can now regain the piece with the routine capture 23 Qxd6. However, after 23 . . . Qxd6 24 Rxd6 Bxg2+ 25 Kxg2 Rxe3 Black is only one pawn down and the presence of double rooks, the active black rook on e3 and White's split kingside pawn gives Black excellent drawing prospects.

Therefore, if possible, White would like a surer winning plan. He sees that with the help of a couple of simple checks he can build up massive strength from a queen + bishop battery:

| 23 Bd4+! | Kf8 |

An immediate mate awaits after 23 . . . Kh6 24 Qh3 mate

| 24 Qf6+ | Kg8 |
| 25 Rfe1! | |

The immediate 25 Qh8+ Kf7 26 Qg7+ allows Black's king to flee to the e-file with 26 . . . Ke6. The text move, bringing into the attack

White's last non-participating piece, prevents the king flight and threatens devastation starting with Qh8+. Defense with 25 . . . Re7 fails to 26 Qh8+ Kf7 27 Qxh7+ Kf8 28 Qh8+! Kf7 29 Qg7+ Ke8 30 Rxe4! Rxe4 31 Qxg6+ followed by 31 Qxe4. Black's choice is only between major evils and the game continuation is "as good" as any.

25 . . .	Qb7
27 Qh8+	Kf7
27 Qxh7+	Ke6
28 Qxb7!	

Black resigns

White, of course, is more than satisfied with the three extra pawns in the ending after 28 . . . Rxb7 29 Rxe4+ Kf7 30 Rxe8.

Correctly keeping the queens on during quite an extended period of middlegame play is marvelously demonstrated from Diagram 111, I. Dorfman – V. Gavrikov, Erevan 1982, after Black's 31st move. White has two pawns for the exchange and thereby a slight material advantage. Also White has the bishop pair in an open position where the bishops have excellent scope. Moreover, White's pawn formation is essentially perfect and his king safe. On the other hand, Black's king position has many holes, partly the result of missing the f-pawn and having instead a somewhat vulnerable e-pawn.

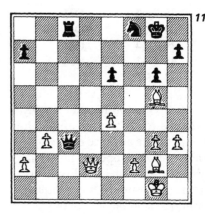

111

White, of course, can now enter a superior endgame with 32 Qxc3. Doing so, however, would rob him of play against Black's vulnerable king. Therefore, to exploit this, White correctly keeps the queens on. This very much increases his winning chances, and since his own king position remains solid as a rock, there is no real risk of losing. "Much to gain, nothing to lose" is the rationale for White's decision.

32 Qe2!	a5
33 Bh6	Nd7
34 Qg4	Kf7
35 Qf4+	Ke8
36 Kh2	

Here and on the following series of moves White basically tries to retain the safe status quo to reach the time control on move 40.

| 36 . . . | Qd3 |
| 37 Qg4 | Qd6 |

38 Qe2	Qc5
39 Be3	Qc6
40 Qg4	Qd6
41 Qe2	Qc6
42 e5!	

After adjournment analysis White is ready to start on a definitive plan: the advance of the e-pawn gains space, opens the King's bishop's diagonal and creates a future opportunity for the queen's bishop to land on d6. All of this will make Black's king insecure—but only because White's queen will always be lurking and ready for the decisive penetration.

42 . . .	Qc7
43 Bd4	Kf7
44 Qf3+	Ke8
45 Qg4	Nf8
46 Bf1!	Rb8
47 Qf3	Qb7
48 Qc3!	

White's bishops do a marvelous job of attacking and defending, while White's queen of course supplies the major power. In order to deflect the danger to his a-pawn, Black is forced to allow White's queen's bishop into d6.

48 . . .	Rd8
49 Bc5	Nd7
50 Bd6	Rc8
51 Qd2!	

51 Qxa5?! Rc2! would allow Black too much counterplay. In a position of maximum strength—such as White has here—there is no need to give the opponent *any* chances.

51 . . .	Qf3
52 Bb5!	Qf5
53 Bc5!	

Both preventing 53 . . . Rc2 and uncovering on Black's knight + king. Now 53 . . . Rxc5? drops the rook after 54 Qxd7+ Kf8 55 Qd6+.

53 . . .	Qf7
54 Qd6!	Kd8
55 Be3	h6
56 h4	Qe7
57 Qd2!	
Black resigns	

He is in a frightful bind and has no satisfactory defense to threats such as 58 Bxh6 (followed by 59 Bg5) and 58 Qxa5.

21

When Complications Should be Avoided

Once you have obtained the superior position, your overriding objective is to retain your advantage. If you can increase it, so much the better, but the minimum requirement is to keep what you have. Often it is necessary to take risks to hope to gain an advantage. However, once the advantage is yours, then take no more risks. In particular, *avoid unnecessary complications.*

When there is the choice between entering a superior endgame or staying in an unclear middlegame, the superior endgame should always be preferred. In this chapter you will learn when to avoid complications.

A typical example is shown from Diagram 112, K. Strzelecki – Schodeberg, European Junior Championship, Groningen 1980/81, after Black's 12th move (1 e4 c6 2 d4 d5 3 Nc3 dxe4 4 Nxe4 Nf6 5 Nxf6+ gxf6 6 Ne2 Bg4 7 Qd3 e6? 8 Ng3 e5 9 Be3 Nd7 10 f4 exf4 11 Bxf4 Qe7+ 12

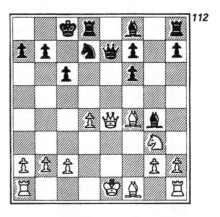

Qe4 0-0-0). It is easy to recognize that White has a significant structural advantage: he has a sound 4 pawn vs. 3 pawn majority on the queenside, whereas Black's extra pawn on the kingside is one of isolated doubled f-pawns. Black's only chance is in the middlegame because White's king is as yet uncastled. Therefore White's clear, simple, consistent plan is to exchange queens with *13 Qxe7! Bxe7* and then to complete minor piece development with *14 Be2!*. White then has a large advantage in an "ideal" endgame, i.e. an endgame where he has clear strengths and no weaknesses.

Instead, the youthful white player preferred complications. A marvelously interesting game resulted, *but without an advantage for White* and it ended a draw. The actual game course:

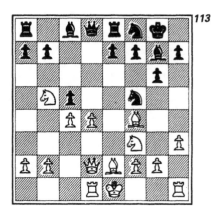

13	Bd3?	Qb4+
14	c3	Qxb2
15	0-0	Be6
16	Rab1	Qa3
17	c4	Nc5!
18	Rxb7!!	Nxe4
19	Rc7+	Kb8
20	Rb1+	Bb4!
21	Bxe4	Rxd4
22	Rxc6+	Kb7
23	Rb3	Rxe4!
24	Rc7+	Kb8
25	Nxe4	Qa4
26	Nc5	Qa5
27	Rxb4+	Ka8
28	Nd3	Qxa2
29	Be3	Rc8
	Draw	

Different in nature but also of great practical importance is the type of position shown in Diagram 113, P. Littlewood – J. Mestel, Hastings 1981/82, after Black's 13th move (1 d4 Nf6 2 Nf3 g6 3 c4 Bg7 4 Nc3 0-0 5 e4 c6?! 6 e5 Ne8 7 Bf4 d6

8 h3 Nd7 9 exd6 Nxd6 10 Be2 Re8 11 Qd2! Nf5 12 Rd1 c5 13 Nb5! Nf8). White has used his central superiority as a springboard for an effective attack against the c7 square. He now has two logical looking choices:

1. Winning a pawn in an endgame = the right way

14	dxc5!	Qxd2+
15	Bxd2	Ne6
16	b4!	

White has a massive grip on the queenside, is a pawn up and secure enough. *This simple way is the correct way* and was suggested after the game by Mestel.

2. Winning the exchange for a pawn in a middlegame = the wrong way

14 Nc7?	Nxd4!
15 Nxe8	

After 15 Nxa8 e5 Black already has a strong center and the a8 knight will not escape.

15 . . .	Qxe8

Black now has a very valuable central pawn for the exchange. In such a middlegame position this is sufficient compensation. *This complicated way is the wrong way.* In the game White went on to lose more time and Black quickly built up an overwhelming center and went on to win as follows:

16 Ne5?	f6
17 Nd3	b6
18 0-0	Bb7
19 Be3	e5
20 Rfe1	Rd8
21 Bxd4	Rxd4!
22 Bf1	Ne6
23 f3	h5
24 b4	cxb4
25 Qxb4	Bf8
26 Qc3	Qd7
27 Kh1	Kh7
28 Qc2	Bc6
29 Qb1	Ba4
30 Rd2	Bh6
31 Rb2	Bf8

32 Nf2	Ba3
33 Ne4	Kg7
34 Rf2	Bc6
35 Nc3	Bc5
36 Nb5	Rh4
37 Rd1	Nd4
38 Nxd4	Rxd4!
39 Re1	Rh4
40 Rd1	Rd4
41 Re1	h4
42 Rb2	Qd6
43 Rb3	e4!
44 fxe4	Qe5
45 Rbe3	Bd6
46 g3	Rxe4!
47 Qxe4	

47 Rxe4 loses to 47 . . . Qxg3 48 Qb2 (48 R1e2 f5) 48 . . . Qxe1

47 . . .	Bxe4+
48 Rxe4	Qxg3
49 R4e2	Bb4
50 Rd1	Qf3+
51 Kh2	Bd6+!
52 Kg1	Bc5+
53 Kh2	Qg3+
54 Kh1	Qg1
Mate	

An excellent example of what befalls those who want too much too soon is shown from Diagram 114, G. Flear – R. Hess, Lugano 1983, after Black's 23rd move. White here has the permanent advantages of the superior center and the bishop pair in a fairly open position. However, the presence of

(see following diagram)

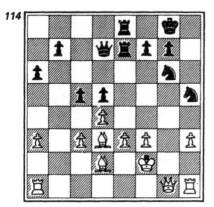

114

all of the heavy pieces, Black's pressure along the e-file and the somewhat exposed location of White's king makes the realization of white's advantages in the middlegame uncertain.

The safe, logical and full of potential approach is to minimize Black's chances and head for the endgame with 24 Qg4!. After 24 . . . Nf6 25 Qxd7 Nxd7 (or 25 . . . Rxd7) 26 a4! White has excellent potential for play on the queenside, center or even the kingside. On the other hand, Black is stymied because the endgame nature of the position has denied him realistic chances for attacking White's king. "Much to gain; nothing to lose" is the correct evaluation of White's chances after 26 a4!.

However, in the game White wanted more — and came up with a negative result:

24 Qg5?!

International master (now Grandmaster) Flear comments here: "I was rather obsessed with mating him and underestimated his resources."

24 . . .   Nf6
25 h4

Grabbing the pawn with 25 Bxg6?! fxg6 26 Qxg6 Rf7 gives Black dangerous counterplay along the e- and f-files. Moreover, the light squares in White's position are then weak.

25 . . .   Qd6!

The situation now is unclear. After the consistent 26 h5 Black can defend by 26 . . . Nh7! 27 Qg2 Ngf8 28 Rag1 Qh6. Being dissatisfied with this, White again wants more and blunders.

26 Rag1?   cxd4
27 exd4

After 27 cxd4, the simple 27 . . . Qxa3 is very strong. But after the text move Black plays an attractive combination.

27 . . .   Ne4+!
28 fxe4   dxe4
29 h5

After 29 Bc4 e3+ 30 Bxe3 Rxe3 31 Qxg6 Black wins with 31 . . . Qf4+ (Flear).

29 . . .	exd3
30 hxg6	Re2+
31 Kf3	fxg6!
32 Bf4	Rf8
33 Rh4	

White is defenseless, since the "desirable" 33 Qh4 is refuted by 33 . . . Rxf4+! 34 Qxf4 Rf2+

33 . . .	Qc6+
34 Kg3	d2
35 Qc5	Rg2+
36 Rxg2	Qxc5
37 dxc5	d1=Q
38 Rgh2	Qd3+
39 Kf2	Rf5
White resigns	

22

Exchanging Queens When Ahead in Material

You have every right to be very satisfied if you find yourself in a middlegame where you are up material. The next step should be to make sure that you win the game. Since a normal won endgame is always safer than a normal won middlegame your first objective should be to try to reach what I call "a matter of technique endgame". Once you are in such an endgame, then apply the techniques learned in Part II. If a direct approach lets you get the queens off, by all means go for it. A fine example of how a top grandmaster does it is shown from Diagram 115, R. Vaganian– H. Westerinen, Moscow 1982, after Black's 21st move. It is easy enough to see that White is up a healthy pawn and that Black does not have the slightest compensation for it. Yet remembering that "the only thing safer than a safe middlegame is a safe endgame", Vaganian without the slightest bit of "shame" heads for that:

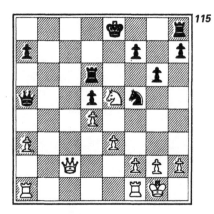

115

22 Qc8+	Qd8
23 Qxd8+!	Rxd8
24 Rfc1	0-0
25 Rc7	a6
26 Rac1	

The first direct benefit of the exchange of queens is that White's rooks dominate the c-file and this soon will be transformed into the domination of the 7th rank. Moreover Black's vulnerable a- and d-pawns are in greater danger with the queens off.

162

26 ...	Rd6
27 Ra7	f6
28 Nd3	Rf7
29 Rc8+	Kg7
30 Rcc7	

Being up material, White follows the principle "exchange pieces".

30 ...	Rxc7
31 Rxc7+	Kf8
32 Nc5!	

And not 32 Rxh7?! since Black after 32 . . . Rb6! wins White's a-pawn and therefore obtains some counterplay.

32 ...	Kg8
33 Rb7	Rc6
34 a4	Nd6
35 Ra7	Rb6
36 g4	h5
37 Rxa6!	

White does not mind giving Black the g-pawn since by getting the rooks off he can capture Black's d-pawn at his leisure.

37 ...	Rxa6
38 Nxa6	hxg4
39 Nc7	Nc4
40 Kg2	Kf7
41 Kg3	f5
42 Kf4!	Ke7

Now White's king penetrates, but Black's position crumbles just as much after 42 . . . Kf6 43 Nxd5+ Ke6 44 e4.

43 Kg5	Kd6
44 Nb5+	Kc6
45 Kxg6	Nb2
46 Nc3	Nd3
47 Kxf5	Nxf2
48 Kf4	
Black resigns	

Since the enemy queen can alway be a source of unwelcome counter-play so too in won endgames it is desirable to exchange it off. Consider now the position of Diagram 116, R. Mascarinas–

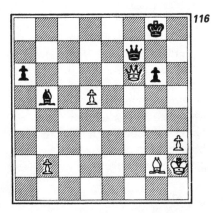

Z. Franco, Medina del Campo 1982, after Black's 49th move. White's queen is actively placed and he can retain an active position with 50 Qe5, but then 50 . . . Bf1! gets the bishops off and the resulting open position gives Black good practical chances for perpetual check. Therefore, again, nothing is as safe as a matter of technique basic endgame:

50 Qxf7+!	Kxf7
51 Kg3	g5
52 Kf3	Bd7
53 Ke4	a5

Otherwise after 54 b4 Black's a-pawn will be fixed on the vulnerable a6 square. Yet it also is vulnerable on a5.

54 Ke5	Ke7
55 d6+	Kd8
56 Kf6	g4
57 hxg4	

A surprising decision, since the general strategy for White is not to exchange pawns. And in point of fact the thematic 57 h4 does win. However, White prefers the simpler text since he has seen that after the bind established with his 58th move he is assured of capturing Black's a-pawn for nothing.

57 . . .	Bxg4
58 Bc6!	Bh3
59 Ke5	Kc8
60 Kd4	a4

Pointless, yet otherwise White plays 61 Kc5, 62 Kb6 and 63 Kxa5.

| 61 Bxa4 | Kb7 |
| 62 Kc5 | Bg2 |

63 b4	Bf3
64 Bd7	
Black resigns	

The general principle is that when you are up material and you see some chances for counterplay by the opponent, that you go for the queen exchange. A clear execution of this is shown from Diagram 117,

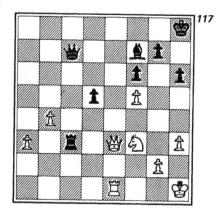

117

H. Bastian–V. Korchnoi, Baden-Baden 1982, after Black's 39th move. White no doubt has a theoretically won position, yet Black's queen + rook are in a position to menace White's king and, moreover, Black with a . . . d4 pawn sacrifice could develop his bishop actively on d5. Wanting to make sure that his famous opponent does not escape, White quite correctly plays:

40 Qe7!	Qxe7
41 Rxe7	Bh5
42 Nd4!	

White does not have to worry about losing back his pawn, since he can recapture Black's d-pawn at his leisure. Also 42 . . . Rd3 is no problem since White has 43 Ne6!

42 . . .	Rxa3
43 Rd7!	Ra8
44 b5!	Rb8
45 b6!	Rxb6
46 g4	

And so White has trapped and wins Black's bishop (46 . . . Rb4 47 Ne6 etc.). Such a plan would be suicidal with queens on, but in an endgame it is riskless. White wins the resultant endgame without any difficulties. After all, a piece is a piece is a piece . . .

46 . . .	Bxg4
47 hxg4	h5
48 gxh5	Rb4
49 Rxd5	Kh7
50 Kg2	Kh6
51 Ne6	Rb7
52 Rd3!	Kxh5
53 Rg3	Kh4
54 Rg6	Rb3
Black resigns	

Black here overstepped the time limit. White's most forcing win is 55

Rxg7 Rb5 56 Kf3! Rxf5+ 57 Nf4 followed by 58 Rg4 mate.

In our next example, Diagram 118, A Lukin–A. Ermolinsky,

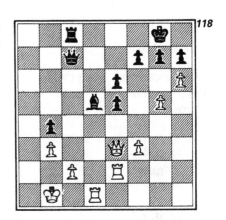

USSR 1982, after Black's 31st move White seems to have both a material advantage and an attack. Yet the question of the attack is not that clear since Black's pressure along the c-file, his well placed bishop and the open a-file also give Black very real practical attacking chances Moreover, a "safe looking" move like 32 Rd3?! leads to an unclear position after 32 . . . gxh6! 33 gxh6 f6, since Black's center now is very strong. Therefore, again the clear way is the endgame:

32 Qxe5!	Qxe5
33 Rxe5	Bxf3
34 Rd4	Re8

The b-pawn is indefensible (34 . . . Rb8?! 35 Rb5!); thus Black works to mobilize his pawn majority. However, White also obtains connected passed pawns and these must be decisive in the long run.

35 Rxb4

White can slow down the start of Black's counterplay if he first plays 35 hxg7!.

35 . . .	gxh6!
36 Rf4	Bh5
37 gxh6	f5
38 c4	Kf7
39 c5	Kf6
40 Re1	e5
41 Rc4	Bf7
42 Rc3	Bd5
43 c6!	Rc8
44 Rd1	Ke6
45 c7	f4
46 Rc5	Bb7
47 Kc2!	e4
48 Rd8!	e3

The pawns also get stopped after 48 . . . f3 49 Rxc8 Bxc8 50 Kd2 f2 51 Rc1 Ba6 52 Ke3!.

49 Rxc8	Bxc8
50 Kd3	Kd6
51 b4	
Black resigns	

The end could be 51 . . . Ba6+ 52 Ke4 e2 53 Rc1.

If you are ahead significant material but the realization of it is difficult because your opponent is attacking you, then always consider giving back some of your bounty to get the queens off. An excellent example is from Diagram 119, A.

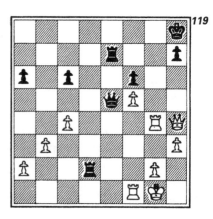

Rodriguez–G. Kuzmin, Minsk 1982, after Black's 41st move. White is two pawns up, but the black rook on d2 is both menacing White's queenside and the king and Black's queen is ready to join in the latter pursuit. Therefore:

42 Qg3!   Qxg3

The mate threat on g8 gives black no real choice since 42 . . . Qc5+ 43 Kh1 Re8 44 Qc7 is very strong for White.

43 Rxg3   a5

Recapturing a pawn with 43 . . . Rxa2 allows White's second rook to be activated decisively after 44 Rd1, e.g. 44 . . . h5 45 Rd6 Rg7 46 Kh2! with a won endgame.

44	a4	Re8
45	Kh2	Re5
46	Rff3	Rd8
47	Rd3!	Rxd3
48	Rxd3	Kg7

Recovering one pawn with 48 . . . Rxf5 leads to loss of another one after 49 Rd6 c5 50 Ra6.

49	g4	h5
50	Kg3	hxg4
51	hxg4	Re1
52	Kf4	Kh6
53	Rh3+	Kg7
54	g5!	Rf1+
55	Kg4	Rg1+
56	Rg3	Rd1
57	g6	Rd4+
58	Kf3	Rh4
59	Ke3	Rh5
60	Rf3	Rh4
61	Kd2!	

Freeing the way for the rook, e.g. 61 . . . c5 62 Rd3!.

61	. . .	Rh5
62	Kd3	Rh4
63	Kc3!	Rh1
64	Kd4	
Black resigns		

The position of Diagram 120, D. Donchev–J. Lechtinsky, Trnava

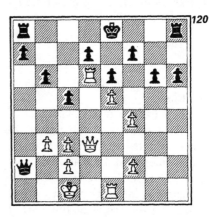

1982, after White's 24th move, even though considerably more complicated than the previous one, requires the same theme as before: returning some of the material advantage to exchange queens. Black here is two healthy pawns up and, moreover, White's kingside pawn formation is poor. Yet White's heavy artillery is in a position to attack and Black's queen is caught behind enemy lines. Greed will be punished, e.g. 24 . . . 0-0-0? 25 Re4! with the frightful threat of 26 Ra4. The correct way is to *quickly* get the queen back. Therefore Black plays:

24	. . .	c4!
25	Qxc4	Qa3+
26	Kd2	Qc5!
27	Qxc5	

Keeping the queens on is no better: 27 Qe4 Rc8 or 27 Qd3 Qxf2+, with Black up material in a good position.

27 ...   **bxc5**

With a vastly superior endgame for Black.

Black has the dual advantages of an extra pawn and the passed h-pawn. White decides to eliminate the former, but the latter defeats him. The further course of this endgame is interesting, but since it is outside the scope of this part, I shall give it without further comments:

28	Ra6	Ke7
29	Rea1	h5!
30	Rxa7	Rxa7
31	Rxa7	h4
32	Ra1	h3
33	Ke3	h2
34	Rh1	Rh3+
35	f3	Rh4!

36	b4	Kd8!
37	b5	Kc7
38	Kf2	Rxf4
39	Rxh2	Rf5!
40	Rh7	g5
41	Rg7	c4
42	Kg3	Rxe5
43	Rxf7	Rxb5
44	f4	gxf4+
45	Kxf4	Kc6!
46	Ke3	Rh5
47	Rf4	d5
48	Kd2	Rh2+
49	Kd1	Kd6
50	Rf3	Ke5
51	Rf1	Kd6
52	Rf6	Ke7!
53	Rf1	e5
54	Rf5	Ke6
55	Rg5	Kf6!
56	Rg8	Kf5
57	Rg1	Rf2!
58	Rh1	Kf4
59	Rh5	Rg2!
60	Rh4+	Kf3
61	Rh5	e4!

White resigns

23

Exchanging Queens is the Right Approach

In most middlegame positions there is, of course, material equality. Your own position can either be safe or not-so-safe. What are the benchmarks to use when considering an exchange of queens? These will be discussed for both of the above types of positions. But always keep in mind that you do not want to exchange queens *if* this decreases your winning chances. This chapter will show when to exchange queens. The next chapter will discuss when not to do so.

1. Your position is safe

Since your own position is safe fear is not a factor in deciding whether to exchange queens. The overriding consideration is whether you have a better chance of progress with the queens off. A good starting point for this discussion is Diagram 121, M. Matulovic – Z. Klaric, Vinkovci 1982, after

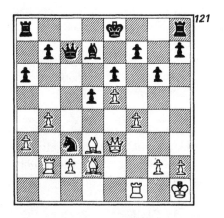

Black's 25th move. White has a nice safe middlegame position, but what to do with it? Moreover, the queen's rook stands clumsily on b2 and the attempt to improve its location by playing 26 Rb3 is met by 26 . . . Na4, followed by 27 . . . Nb6 and 28 . . . Nc4. However, there is an opportunity to enter an endgame with significantly increased winning chances:

26 Qc5!   **Qxc5**

Black has no choice because White has the double threat on the queen and on the knight (26 . . . Nb5?? 27 Bxb5 Qxc5 28 Bxd7+).

27 bxc5

Notice how immediately the clumsy rook on b2 has been transformed into a power along the b-file. Black cannot prevent the rook's incursion, because 27 . . . Nb5 fails to 28 a4.

27 . . .	Na4
28 Rxb7	Nxc5
29 Rc7	Rc8

There also is no relief in 29 . . . Nxd3 30 cxd3 Rc8 since after 31 Rfc1 White's remaining rook will be the active one.

30 Rxc8+	Bxc8
31 Be2!	Kd7
32 Rb1	

Here too White's rook is master of the queenside. The bishop pair powerfully eyes both sides and over-all White has a significant advantage.

32 . . .	Kc6
33 Ba5	Nd7
34 Rb3	Kc5
35 Kg1	g5?!

This attempt at counterplay should boomerang immediately because of 36 fxg5! Nxe5 37 Bb4+! Kc6 38 Bc3 Kd6 39 Rb6+ Kc7 40 Bxe5+. Instead, White, being short of time, decides to play safe.

36 g3	gxf4
37 gxf4	f6
38 Bb4+	Kd4?!

Black can hold out longer after 38 . . . Kc6 39 Rc3+ Kb7 40 Bd6, though his prospects remain bleak.

39 exf6	Ke4
40 Be7	Kxf4
41 f7	
Black resigns	

The passed pawn will win at least a piece.

Also instructive is Black's reasoning in Diagram 122, L. Miagmasuren – W. Browne, Lucerne

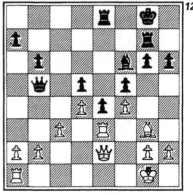
122

Olympiad 1982, after White's 26th move. Black has a very favorable middlegame because of the protected passed e-pawn and the superior bishop. Still, to make further progress Black will have to start undermining White's pawn chains with breaks via . . . g5 and . . . b4. The successful execution of them is just so much more certain with White's queen off the board. Therefore, Black plays:

26 . . .	Qxe2!
27 Rxe2	Kf7
28 Kf2	b5!
29 Ke3	Rc8!

Black is now ready for his queenside break. White cannot go for counterplay with 30 a4?! because of 30 . . . b4! 31 cxb4 Rc4 (Browne) and Black has a winning advantage.

30 Be1	g5!
31 a4	b4!
32 cxb4	gxf4+
33 Kxf4	Ke6!
34 Ke3	

After 34 Bc3 Browne gives 34 . . . Rcg8 35 b5 (35 g3?? Bg5 mate) 35 . . . Rxg2 as Black's clearest win.

| 34 . . . | f4+! |
| 35 Kd2 | |

After 35 Kxf4 Bxd4 there is no reasonable defense to 36 . . . Rf8 mate.

35 . . .	Bxd4
36 Kd1	Rgc7
37 b5	Be3
38 Bc3	d4
39 Rxe3	

Panic in time pressure. Of course neither is there a defense after 39 Bd2 Bxd2 40 Rxd2 Kd5 41 a5 e3.

| 39 . . . | fxe3! |
| White resigns | |

A more unbalanced position and semi-blockaded in nature is shown from Diagram 123, P. Benko – R. Delaune, Valley Forge International 1984, after Black's 19th move. White has a clear advantage and his position is absolutely safe.

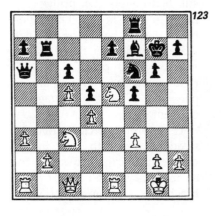

Still, the "age old" question is: how best to play for the win? Grandmaster Benko has discussed this position in *Chess Life* and given his thinking as follows:

"White has an obvious positional advantage because he dominates the e-file due to Black's backward e-pawn. How to proceed from here? I suspected that Black's plan was to get rid of my knight on e5; I, in turn, was considering 20 b4. How would these two ideas resolve themselves? I looked at the possible line 20 b4 Nd7 21 b5 cxb5 22 c6 Nxe5 23 cxb7, but realized that 23 . . . Nd3 24 Qe3 Nxe1 25 Qe5+ Qf6 gives Black sufficient counterplay.

Unhappy with this, I searched for an improvement in that line. At first, 22 Nxf7 (instead of 22 c6) 22 . . . Rxf7 23 Nxd5 Nb8 24 Nf4 looked great, but somehow I still had doubts. On principle, I hated to trade my good knight on e5 for the bad bishop on f7. Then there was the fact that Black is not forced to play 20 . . . Nd7 right away; he can prepare to play it at a more advantageous moment.

Therefore, I decided that instead of trying to cash in my middlegame chips, to strive for an endgame where I could exploit Black's weak pawn formation."

There are just two things that I can add:

(1) White's queen is not needed for the above goal; as a matter of fact, it is easier to proceed without it, and (2) The theme throughout the coming endgame is that a white knight absolutely dominates Black's impotent bishop.

| 20 Qc2! | Nd7 |
| 21 Qd3 | Qxd3 |

Obviously the queen exchange is forced.

22 Nxd3	Kf6
23 Re2	Rc8
24 Rae1	Nf8
25 Ne5	Bg8
26 b4	Ne6
27 Rd2	Nd8
28 f4	

Forever blockading the e-pawn. White now does have to make sure, however, that Black's knight is not allowed to get to e4.

28 . . .	h6
29 g3	g5
30 Kf2	Be6
31 Rde2	Bg8
32 Rb1!	

Preparing the logical b5 break so as to turn the c5 pawn into a protected passed one. Then, for practical purposes, White has a

pawn advantage since Black's hopelessly blocked e-pawn is useless for
offensive purposes.

32	. . .	a6
33	Na4	e6
34	Nb6	R8c7
35	a4	Bf7
36	b5	axb5
37	axb5	cxb5
38	Rxb5	Ra7
39	Rbb2	Be8
40	Ra2	Nc6
41	Nxc6	Bxc6
42	Reb2	Rxa2
43	Rxa2	g4
44	Kg2!	Kg6
45	h4!	gxh3+

Otherwise, with the kingside now
safely blockaded, White's king will
penetrate into Black's queenside
for the win.

46	Kxh3	Kh5
47	Re2	Re7
48	Nc8	Rc7
49	Nd6	Bd7
50	Rb2	e5

Desperation, but otherwise
White wins with the prosaic 51 Rb7,
followed by queening his pawn.

51	fxe5	f4+
52	Kg2	fxg3
53	Kxg3	Kg5
54	Rb7!	Rxb7
55	Nxb7	h5

56	Nd8	h4+
57	Kh2	Bc8
58	c6	Kg6
59	c7	

Black resigns

The next example, Diagram 124,
G. Kasparov – S. Gligoric, Lucerne
Olympiad 1982, after Black's 28th
move, shows a position which has
features of both an endgame and a
middlegame. White's middlegame
advantage is that he has the bishop
pair in a fairly open position.

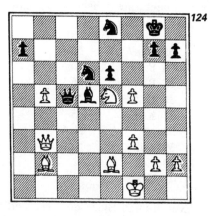

However, the somewhat cluttered
nature of the position and the Black
queen's powerful location makes
further progress in the middlegame
uncertain. Therefore, Kasparov
switches into a pure endgame:

29	Qa3!	Qxa3
30	Bxa3	exf5
31	Bc5	

The first immediate result of the exchange of queens is that Black's a-pawn is extremely vulnerable.

| 31 . . . | Nc8 |
| 32 Nc6! | Kf7 |

Black gives up the pawn voluntarily, rather than allow the variation 32 . . . Bxc6 33 Bc4+! Bd5 (33 . . . Kh8 34 bxc6 is also hopeless since Black's king can not participate in helping to stop the c-pawn) 34 Bxd5+ Kh8 35 Be6 Ned6 36 Kf2 (Kasparov) and White's king will penetrate decisively into Black's position.

33 Nxa7	Nxa7
34 Bxa7	Ke6
35 Bd4	g6
36 Kf2	Nd6
37 Ke3	g5
38 g3	Nc4+
39 Kd3	Nd6
40 Kc3	f4
41 Kb4!	

Even though Black does succeed in exchanging off two kingside pawns, White's active king will be the decisive factor. Kasparov plays the rest of the game very accurately and powerfully.

41 . . .	fxg3
42 hxg3	h5
43 Bf2	Nf5
44 f4!	gxf4
45 gxf4	Ng7

Or 45 . . . h4 46 Bg4 Kf6 47 Kc5 Bg2 48 b6 Ng3 49 Be1! (Kasparov).

46 Kc5	Bg2
47 Bd4	h4
48 Bxg7	h3
49 Bg4+	Ke7
50 Bxh3	Bxh3
51 Kb6!	
Black resigns	

The conclusion could be 51 . . . Bf1 52 Kc6 Kd8 53 b6 Bg2+ 54 Kd6 Be4 55 f5! etc.

2. Your position is not-so-safe

Many middlegame positions do contain clear dangers for the superior side. Some positions are only somewhat unsafe, whereas others very clearly require considerable care and skill not to run one's chess ship onto the shoals. In such cases, the attraction of a queen exchange of course increases. Nevertheless, you want to do so only if your winning chances are not compromised.

There even are times when the exchange of queens is the *only* way to retain an advantage. Consider Diagram 125, F. Gobet – V. Hort, Biel 1982, after Black's 15th move (After 1 e4 c5 2 Nf3 Nc6 3 Nc3 d6 4

(see following diagram)

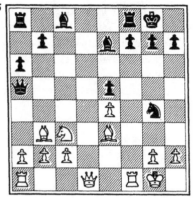

d4 cxd4 5 Nxd4 Nf6 6 Bc4 Qb6 7
Ndb5 a6 8 Be3 Qa5 9 Nd4 e6 10 0-0
Be7 11 Bb3 0-0 12 f4 Nxd4 13 Bxd4
e5 14 fxe5 dxe5 15 Be3 Ng4?). With
his last move Black has gone on an
adventurous sortie where by attacking White's queen's bishop Black
wants to score on the g1 – a7
diagonal. White cannot dish out any
punishment in the middlegame
since 16 Rxf7? is refuted by
16 . . . Rxf7 17 Qf1 Nh6! 18 Bxh6
Be6! 19 Bxe6 Qb6+ (Gobet), while
16 Nd5?! Bc5 yields Black dark
square superiority. However, Black
had overlooked the strength of
White's response:

16 Qd5!   Qxd5

The double threat on a5 and f7
forces Black to exchange.

17 Nxd5   Bd6
18 Bb6!

Already it is clear that White has
a bind on the center and the queenside. Notice how irrelevant Black's
knight now is on g4.

18 . . .	Be6
19 Rad1	Rac8
20 h3	Rc6
21 hxg4	Bxd5
22 Rxd5	Rxb6
23 Rfd1!	Bb8
24 Rd7	

White has the dual advantages of
the active rooks and superior
bishop. The absence of queens
means that White's king position is
secure enough.

24 . . .	Ba7
25 Kh2	Rh6+
26 Kg3	Rf6
27 g5	Rf4
28 Kh3	g6
29 g3!	

With some fine maneuvers White
has safeguarded his king and now is
ready to use his attacking power. If
now 29 . . . Rxe4, White wins with
30 Rf1 Re3 31 Bxf7+ Kh8 32 Bd5!
Rxf1 33 Rd8+ Kg7 34 Rg8 Mate
(Gobet).

29 . . .	Rf2
30 Rxb7	Bd4
31 c3	Be3
32 Kg4!	Kg7
33 Rdd7	h5+

34 gxh6+	Bxh6
35 Bd5	Bd2
36 c4	Be1
37 c5!	Rg2
38 Rb3	Kh6
39 Rxf7	
Black resigns	

For maximum success, it is important to combine technical knowledge with a mind that is always creative. Already in the previous example we saw the strength of an unexpected queen exchange. An even more surprising example is shown from Diagram 126, A. Adorjan – Vl. Kovacevic, Sarajevo 1982, after White's 38th move. It is easy to see that Black has a strong attacking position.

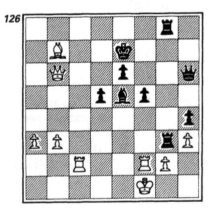

Conventional wisdom would have Black keeping the queens on so that he can "attack better". Yet a more

sophisticated look at Diagram 126 shows that White is just able to defend everything and, moreover, his queen obviously is a menace to Black's not-so-safe king. Therefore Black takes care of both aspects with:

| 38 . . . | Qe3! |
| 39 Qxe3 | |

Black's queen can not really be allowed to remain on the dominant e3 square, yet the coming endgame is also lost.

39 . . .	Rxe3
40 Rfe2	Rxe2
41 Rxe2	Kd6
42 b4	Rg3!
43 Ra2	Rb3!
White resigns	

White actually played 44 Bc8 and then resigned in view of 44 . . . Bb2.

In Diagram 127, O. Averkin – Y. Razuvaev, Sochi 1982, after Black's 31st move, White has the dual advantages of a powerful center and control of the open d-file. Yet—for a middlegame position—White's king is somewhat precariously placed on f3. White now turns the middlegame disadvantage into the endgame

(see following diagram)

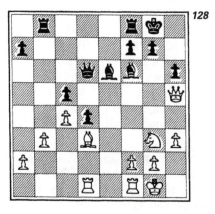

127

Hallucination, though the normal 42 . . . Rxd7 43 exd7 Rd8 is also hopeless after 44 gxh7+ Kxh7 45 Rd2 Kg6 46 Rd6! Kf7 47 Kd5 (Averkin).

43 Rxd1
Black resigns

In Diagram 128, L. Miagmasuren – E. Torre, Lucerne Olympiad 1982, after White's 20th move, Black has two advantages: a passed protected d-pawn and the bishop

advantage of having the well centralized king by playing:

32	Qd5+!	Qxd5
33	Rxd5	Rb1
34	Re2	Rf1+
35	Ke3	Rc8
36	Rd7!	Rg1

To prevent 37 Rg2. However, now White can mobilize his center pawns.

37	e5!	Re8
38	e6	g6
39	Ke4!	Rc1
40	Kd5!	Rc8
41	fxg6	Rd1+?!

Black is still blitzing away after the time control has been reached. However, White's win is equally certain after 41 . . . hxg6 42 Kd6.

42 Ke4   hxg6??

128

pair in a fairly open position. Yet White's queen + bishop + knight are poised to menace Black's king and thus the exploitation of Black's advantage is uncertain. Therefore, Black works to exchange off White's queen so that he can then start "doing his own thing", without risk of counterplay by White:

20	...	Qe5!
21	Qf3	Bg5!
22	Rfe1	Qf4!
23	Qxf4	Bxf4
24	Ne4	Rfc8
25	g3	Bg5
26	Nxg5	hxg5
27	Kg2	Re8!

Black still has the protected passed d-pawn; the advantage of the two bishops has been transformed into that of the superior bishop.

28	g4	Bd7
29	Kg3	a5
30	h4	gxh4+
31	Kxh4	Kf8
32	Rxe8+	Rxe8
33	Kg3	Bc6
34	a3	Rb8
35	Rb1	Ke7
36	Kf4	Kd6
37	Bc2	Rh8!

Notice how in this endgame Black's pieces have a free hand since they do not have to worry about their king.

38	Kg3	g5
39	Re1	Rb8
40	Rb1	Bd7
41	Bd3	Be6
42	Kf3	Rh8
43	b4?	

White here is in no position for such activity. Torre gives as the

main line 43 Kg3 Rh4! 44 f3 Rh8! 45 b4 cxb4 46 axb4 Rb8! 47 c5+ Kc6 48 Be4+ Bd5 49 bxa5 Rxb1 50 Bxb1 Kb5! with a large edge for Black but some drawing chances for White.

43	...	Rh3+
44	Ke4	Bd7!
45	bxc5+	

It's mate after 45 b5 Bc8! 46 b6 f5+! 47 gxf5 Bb7.

45	...	Kxc5
46	Be2	Rxa3
	White resigns	

A picture perfect demonstration of exploiting your opponent's weaknesses while making sure that your own weaknesses are no problem is shown in Diagram 129, C. van Dyck – D. Eisen, USA Correspondence 1979–82, after Black's 20th move. White's advantages are: he has control of the d-file, a bishop that can

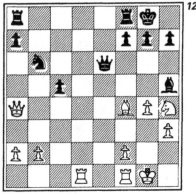

menace Black's queenside pawns and play against Black's vulnerable isolated a- and c-pawns. Yet White's rather open kingside pawn formation makes it doubtful that he can concentrate on exploiting these factors. Therefore, he plays:

| 21 Qb3!! | Qxb3 |

No better is 21 . . . c4 22 Qe3! and worse is 21 . . . Qf6 22 Bg3 Bg6 23 Rd6 Qe7 24 Rxg6!.

| 22 axb3 | Bg6 |
| 23 Nxg6 | fxg6?! |

This will lead to a permanent weakness on g7. Better is 23 . . . hxg6. White's doubled b-pawns are not a real weakness because Black cannot get at them. Note that throughout the coming endgame White's bishop towers over Black's knight.

24 Be3	Rac8
25 Ra1	Rf7
26 Rfc1	Rfc7
27 Ra5	Nd7

Worse is 27 . . . c4 28 bxc4 Rxc4 29 R1a1 Rb4 30 Rxa7 Rxb2 31 Bd4.

28 b4!	cxb4
29 Rxc7	Rxc7
30 Rxa7	Rxa7
31 Bxa7	Kf7
32 Bd4	

White's bishop obviously has a lot more scope than the knight. Moreover, in such an endgame White's advanced kingside pawns are even an advantage since they help to gain space there.

32 . . .	Nf6
33 Kg2	Ke6
34 Bc5	b3
35 Kf3	Kd5
36 Bf8	Ne8
37 Ke3	Kc4
38 f3!	

Putting Black in virtual zug-zwang. After 38 . . . Kd5 White wins with 39 Bb4 Nc7 40 Bc3 Ne6 41 f4! followed by f5 (van Dyck).

38 . . .	h6
39 h4	h5
40 Ke4!	Nf6+
41 Kf4	hxg4
42 fxg4	Ne8
43 Kg5	

White now walks in on the fatally weakened kingside.

43 . . .	Kd3
44 Kxg6	Kc2
45 Kf7	Nf6
46 Bxg7	Nxg4
47 h5	Kb1
48 Kg6	
Black resigns	

24

When Exchanging Queens is Wrong

Nothing good comes easily. A good middlegame means that you have worked hard and successfully in the earlier stages of the game. Therefore, there is some risk that somewhere along the line in the middlegame, you may feel that the time has come to be able to relax. I mean, why continue in the middlegame when there is the opportunity to simplify by entering into the endgame?

In itself such thinking is not harmful—as long as you do not make the wrong decision. But surely you do not want to simplify at the cost of decreasing your chances of success. To guard against the wrongful exchange of queens, always ask yourself: what is the *essence* of the position? In other words, why do I have the advantage in this middlegame? This line of reasoning will prevent you from making many wrong decisions.

The most extreme examples of incorrect exchanging occur when you go from a superior to an inferior position. An excellent first

example is Diagram 130, K. Honfi – V. Jansa, Trnava 1982, after Black's 23rd move. For the sacri-

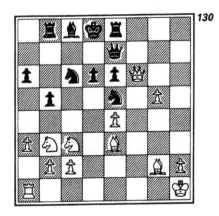

ficed exchange, White has a bishop plus two pawns and therefore a slight material advantage. Moreover, White has attacking prospects against Black's in-the-centre King and has connected passed pawns on the kingside. White's most logical move to retain his advantage is the straightforward 23 Qf4!. Less logical, but sufficient for approximate equality is 23 Qxe7+. Instead,

White played the absolutely illogical:

24	Nd4?!	Nxd4
25	Bxd4??	

The spoiling of the pawn formation is prevented by 25 Qxe7+.

25	. . .	Qxf6!
26	gxf6	Rf8
27	Rf1	Rb7!

What a complete turn of events! Not only is Black's king absolutely safe, but White's isolated f- and h-pawns are weak and vulnerable to attack by Black's rooks. Moreover, White's knight and king's bishop are without scope and his rook has to worry about protecting the f-pawn. It is Black who now has a significant advantage.

28	Be3	Rh7!
29	Kg1	Kc7
30	Bg5	Rh5!
31	h4	Ng6
32	Bf3	Rhh8
33	Kf2	

Already something has to give. The obvious 33 h5 fails to 33 . . . Ne5 with the dual threats of 34 . . . Nxf3 followed by 35 . . . Rxh5 and 34 . . . Rhg8.

33	. . .	Nxh4
34	Be2	Ng6

35	Ke3	Ne5
36	b3	Rh3+
37	Kd2	Bd7
38	Nd1	Bc6
39	Nf2	Rh2
40	Bf4	Rh4
41	Bg3	Rh7
42	Bxe5?!	

According to Jansa, drawing chances were offered only by 42 Nd3! Nxd3 43 cxd3 e5 44 d4! Rh3 45 Rf3.

42	. . .	dxe5
43	Ng4	Kd6
44	Ke3	Rh3+
45	Bf3	Be8!
46	Ke2	Bh5
47	Rd1+	Kc7
48	Nxe5	Bxf3+
49	Nxf3	Rxf6

With the fall of White's pride—the f-pawn—White is left with material and positional inferiority and loses routinely enough.

50	Rd3	Rg6
51	Kf2	Rhg3
52	Ne1	Rxd3
53	Nxd3	a5!
54	Nb2	Rh6!
55	Ke2	Rh1
56	a4	Rb1
57	Nd1	bxa4
58	bxa4	Kd6
59	Nc3	Ra1
60	Kd2	Kc5

61 Kd3	Ra3
62 Kd2	e5
63 Ne2	Rxa4
White resigns	

The turnaround in the result is not as drastic from Diagram 131, I. Farago – I. Radulov, Baille Hercu-lane 1982, after White's 29th move, yet the same idea applies. Partly in

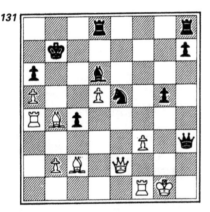

131

jest we can say that both sides stand badly, since the respective kings must feel very uncomfortable. On an immediate basis, however, it is Black who is a move ahead in his attack and this is both the essence of the position and of Black's advantage. Therefore the only con-sistent plan (and move) for Black is to continue the attack with 29 . . . g4! and this both retains and safeguards his advantage. Instead, Black, starting to feel too uncom-fortable, played:

29 . . .	Qg3+?
30 Qg2	Qxg2+
31 Kxg2	Bxb4
32 Rxb4+	Kc7
33 Rd1!	

Now it is White who has the advantage. His king is safe, both rooks are active, the bishop is a powerful minor piece and the d-pawn is a strong and safe passed pawn.

33 . . .	Rhf8
34 Be4	Rb8
35 d6+	Kd7
36 Bf5+	Kc6
37 Be4+	Kd7
38 Bf5+	

Short of time, White satisfies himself with the draw. Subsequent-ly Farago demonstrated that after the correct 38 Rb6!, Black's only defensive resource is 38 . . . Rxb6 39 axb6 Nd3!, with White con-tinuing to retain his advantage.

38 . . .	Kc6
39 Be4+	
Draw	

The second worst thing that can happen because of an incorrect ex-change of queens is that you fail to gain an immediate win. An excel-lent illustration of this is from Dia-gram 132, L. Polugaevsky – J. Nunn, Toluca Interzonal 1982, after

132

Thanks to the active rook and far advanced kingside pawns, Black has enough counterplay for the draw.

45 Rc5	Rb1+
46 Ke2	Rb2+
47 Kd3	Rxg2
48 Rxe5	Rg1!
49 Rg5	

There is no time for 49 Rf5+ Ke7 50 Rxf4?? because of 50 . . . g2! and *Black* wins.

49 . . .	Rf1
50 e5	Rxf3+
51 Ke4	Rf2
52 h4	Rh2

Black's 37th move. The essence of this position quite obviously is that Black's king position is most precarious, because it is open and all three of White's major pieces are so close to it. In such a position you must look for a tactical shot to upset Black's house of cards. And in fact, if you look just a bit, then a two move combination will appear: 38 Rb8! Rxb8 39 Qxe5+ followed by 40 Qxb8+. Such a possibility is neither surprising nor difficult to see—as long as you look for it! Instead, in time pressure White gave up all of his attack for a "measly" pawn:

Also 52 . . . g2 53 h5 f3 54 h6 Re2+ 55 Kxf3 Rxe5! draws.

38 Qxh7+?	Qxh7
39 Rxh7+	Kg8
40 Rbg7+	Kf8
41 Rf7+	Kg8
42 Rfg7+	Kf8
43 Rc7	Rxc7
44 Rxc7	Rb8!

53 Kxf4	Rxh4+
54 Kf5	Ra4
55 Rxg3	Rxa5
56 Rc3	Ra2
57 Ke6	a5
58 Rc8+	Kg7
59 Ke7	a4
60 e6	Rb2!
61 Ra8	a3!
62 Rxa3	Rb7+
63 Kd8	Rb8+
64 Kc7	Rb1!
65 Rf3	Ra1!
66 Rf7+	Kg6
Draw	

Missing an immediate win is dangerous for two reasons. Firstly, that may be the only existing win and if you miss it, it is gone forever. This is what happened in our previous example. The other problem is that once you begin to fail to see the strongest move, this can just feed on itself and even though the position remains promising, you simply cannot get to grips with it again. Therefore, whenever possible, aim for the *immediate* win. Otherwise, what can happen is shown from Diagram 133, D. Rajkovic – P. Scheeren, Plovdiv 1983, after Black's 34th move. Up to here White has played a perfect game.

What is the essence of the position? Is it not that White has a strong attack against Black's king? White's rook controls the 8th rank, his bishop is on a powerful central diagonal, the knight can be brought

to the important e4 square and his queen is powerfully centralized. Therefore, it is quite logical that White has an immediate mating attack starting with the direct 35 Qa8!: 35 . . . g5 36 Rh8+ Kg6 37 Qg8! and there is nothing to be done about the frightful threat of 38 Qh7+ (37 . . . Kh5 38 Bxg7). Instead for some reason (I don't consider being in some time pressure a good enough reason to lose one's basic chess sense) White got cold feet and played:

35 Qxf5?

White banks on the passed d-pawn to be more than sufficient compensation for being a pawn down. His intuition is correct in this, but the bulk of his advantage is gone. Being short of time prevents him from doing something with the remaining part.

35 . . .	Bxf5
36 Nd5	g5!
37 Ne7	Be6
38 Kf2	f3!
39 gxf3	g4
40 f4?	

After this kneejerk reaction White is left with nothing. Necessary is the immediate 40 d7! and White will have some winning

chances after both 40 . . . Rxf3+
41 Ke2 Bxd7 42 Rxd7 Rf7 43 Nd5!
and 40 . . . Bxd7 41 Rxd7 Nf5 42
Bc5 c3! 43 Nd5!.

40 . . .	Rxf4+
41 Ke3	Rf7!
42 Ke4	Rf1!
43 d7	Re1+
44 Be3	Rd1
45 Bd4	Re1+
Draw	

The third reason not to exchange
queens prematurely is that this can
prevent you from exploiting possibilities that exist with the queens
on. Consider now Diagram 134, L.
Kavalek – L. Day, Lucerne Olympiad 1982, after Black's 27th move.

White here has various nice advantages: both rooks have good scope
along their files, both knights have
access to important squares in

Black's position such as c5 and e5,
the dark squares on Black's kingside are permanently weakened,
White has the overall freer and
more active position. To take
advantage of these many factors,
White wants to retain all the firepower that he can. Indicated now is
to continue to increase the pressure
with moves such as 28 Ne5 or 28
Re5. Instead, White, unaccountably, releases much of the pressure
by playing:

| 28 Qh6? | Ra8! |
| 29 Qxg7+ | Kxg7 |

While White has made Black's
kingside more secure, Black has
utilized the time to activate his
queen's rook along the open a-file.
Chances are already equal.

30 Ne5	Ra4
31 Nd7	Rf7
32 Ndc5	Nxc5
33 Nxc5	Rc4!
34 Rxc4	bxc4!
35 b3	cxb3
36 Nxb3	Kf6

Notice how all of White's pressure has disappeared—mostly as a
result of the exchange of queens
and partly because of Black's fine
play.

| 37 Rc1 | Ne6 |
| 38 h4 | Ke7 |

39	Re1	Kd6
40	g3	Rf3
41	Re3	Rf8
Draw		

If White would take a hard-nosed look at the essence of Diagram 135, O. Foisor – M. Suba, Rumania 1984, after Black's 24th move, there is no way that he would make the incorrect decision to exchange queens. Look at the important features of Diagram 135: White's rook on g3 is well placed for the attack,

135

Black's kingside is chronically weak, White is well ahead in development. Moreover, after playing f4 White will chase Black's queen away from the center while getting his own central pawns going, thereby both establishing central superiority and activating his rook on f1. Can it be any clearer that White should remain in the middlegame?

A good, logical plan for White is the one suggested by Foisor *after* the game: 25 Bd3! Rg8 26 f4 Qh5 27 Qc3+ f6 28 Rh3 with an obviously strong attack and large advantage for White. Yet instead, White played the insipid:

25 Qc3?

And was left with less than nothing after . . .

25	...	f5!
26	exf5	Bxf5
27	Bd3	Bxd3
28	Rxd3	Qxc3
29	Nxc3	Ne5
30	Re3	Nc4
31	Re4!	Rxe4
32	Nxe4	Re8
33	f3	Re5
34	Rc1!	Ne3
35	Kf2	Ng4+!
36	Kg3	Ne3
37	Kf2	Ng4+
Draw		

A thoughtful look at Diagram 136, V. Smyslov – B. Ivanovic, Bugojno 1984, after Black's 47th move, should tell us the following: White is a passed d-pawn up, White's Q + R are powerfully placed, Black's king is in real danger from White's pieces, overall there has been a vast reduction in pawns, with only two more remaining on each side. Therefore, to

maximize winning chances White should keep the queens on and play 48 Qd8!. Instead, in view of the somewhat uncomfortable situation of White's king, Smyslov decides to play it easy and safe:

48 Qe6?!	Qxe6
49 dxe6	Re7
50 Kg2	Kg5
51 Kf3	Rb7
52 Rd6	

White's risk of loss here is about zero, yet the small number of pawns remaining has also drastically reduced his winning prospects. Remember that in Diagram 136 White had many advantages; now all that

he has is the extra pawn and this is not enough.

Instead of the text move Smyslov also analyzes 52 Ra4 and shows that Black holds after 52 . . . Kf6!: (a) 53 Re4 Rb3+! 54 Kg2 Ke7; (b) 53 Rxf4+ Kxe6 54 g5 Rb1 55 Rf6+ Ke5 56 Kg2 Ra1 57 Rxg6 Kf5; (c) 53 Kxf4 g5+ 54 Ke4 Kxe6 55 Ra6+ Kf7.

52 . . .	Ra7
53 Ke4	Kxg4
54 Rd1	Kg5
55 Ke5	Ra5+
56 Rd5	Ra2!
57 Rd4	Re2+
58 Re4	Rxe4+
59 Kxe4	Kf6
60 Kd5	

This K + P endgame is also drawn.

60 . . .	Ke7
61 Ke5	f3
62 Kd5	g5
63 Ke5	g4
64 Kf4	g3
65 Kxg3	Kxe6
66 Kxf3	Kf5
Draw	

Part VI
Drawing Inferior Middlegames

Just as it is very nice to find yourself in a superior middlegame, so it is not so nice to be faced with an inferior one. Yet the practical player has to learn to take both of these in stride since he will have plenty of each. To have a successful tournament result a person has to save as many inferior middlegames as possible. This part will give you the necessary tools so that you can make the crucial decisions regarding when to remain in the middlegame and when to hope for salvation in an endgame.

In a superior middlegame you yourself largely control your destiny. In an inferior middlegame—to a certain extent at least—you are at the mercy of fate in the person of your opponent. It is likely that if your opponent plays *perfectly*, he will win. Yet perfection in chess is hard to come by and therefore in real life you do not have to fear such a happening that much. I mean, the chances that every time that your opponent gets a superior middlegame he will handle it with perfection are zero.

Therefore in real life you have plenty of opportunities to help yourself. The first important thing is not to make your practical situation worse by an incorrect exchange of queens. This is considered in depth in Chapter 25. The rest of this part is concerned with what to do: when to remain in the middlegame (Chapter 26), the braking of a kingside attack by exchanging queens (Chapter 27) and exchanging queens to minimize other middlegame troubles (Chapter 28).

25

Making Your Prospects Worse by Exchanging Queens

Because an inferior middlegame is bad enough, you surely do not want to do anything that worsens your situation. The correct approach in practical play is: ALWAYS INCREASE YOUR PRACTICAL CHANCES FOR SUCCESS. There is nothing worse than taking a complicated, albeit inferior middlegame—one where there are real chances that your opponent will misplay it—and voluntarily entering a sufficiently inferior endgame so that your loss is only a matter of time. Not a thing is gained by just *postponing* a loss. What you actually want to aim at is minimizing the certainty of it. If the loss is inevitable, what is the value in losing in 60 moves rather than in 35? When I give simultaneous exhibitions I am always amazed at how many players head for a hopeless endgame, rather than hoping for a middlegame error by me. Well, maybe there is some psychic value in being able to say "I held

out for 55 moves against the grandmaster" rather than having to admit "I got mated in 30". But such behavior when playing your peers has *no* redeeming value!

In this chapter I will illustrate the kind of circumstances where the exchange of queens is totally and hopelessly wrong. If you learn not to do these things, you will be well on your way to learning how to handle inferior middlegames.

The first principle is: *avoid exchanges which are suicidal*. A perfect example is shown from Diagram 137, L. Pliester–J. van der Wiel, Ostend 1983, after Black's 21st move. Black has a clear advantage because his e-pawn is much more valuable than White's extra b-pawn and his minor pieces are actively placed and bear down on White's b2 pawn. White has reason to be unhappy at having played himself into an inferior position so quickly. Still, why not put up a fight? A reasonable plan is 22 Qg4!

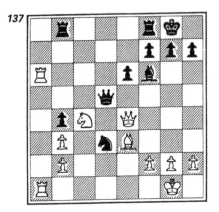

137

White loses heavy material after 26 Nd7 Nxa5 etc. Resignation three moves after a voluntary exchange of queens!

From a practical standpoint what Black does from Diagram 138, J. Nunn–B. Toth, Lugano 1984, after White's 32nd move, is little better.

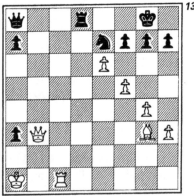

138

Nxb2 23 Rd6 Qb5 24 Nxb2 Bxb2 25 Rad1. White has lost a "useless" pawn, but his remaining pieces stand well, Black's b4 pawn is accessible to an attack by White's bishop and in such a middlegame the realization of Black's extra pawn on the kingside is a far-from-simple task. All in all, White's practical chances for successful resistance are good. Instead, he played:

| 22 Qxd5?? | exd5 |
| 23 Nb6 | d4 |

Notice how "helpfully" White has turned Black's e-pawn into a powerful d-pawn, while ensuring that he has no defense to Black's eventual . . . Nc5, e.g. 24 Bd2 Nc5 25 Bxb4 Nxa6 26 Bxf8 Rxb6.

24 Bc1	Nc5
25 R6a5	Nxb3
White resigns	

We have a most complicated position, where White's king is without cover but, in turn, the advanced e-pawn is a menace to Black. During play such a position is difficult to judge, but it should be fairly clear that Black must use his queen to be able to menace White's king. Almost like a reflex Black should play 32 . . . Qe4! and not worry what "might happen". White then retains some edge with 33 Bh4! but can easily lose his way in the subsequent play. Yet, Black—short of time—plays the "safe":

32 . . .	Qd5??
33 Qxd5	

The only sure thing now is that
Black is suddenly lost. After
33 . . . Rxd5 strong is 34 Bh4!, yet
what Black plays is even worse,
showing that 32 . . . Qd5?? was
just an automatic *wrong* move.

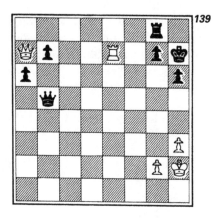

33 . . .	Nxd5?!
34 Rd1	fxe6
35 fxe6	Kf8
36 Bc7!	Rc8
37 Bd6+	Ne7
38 Rf1+	Ke8
39 Rf7	Ng6
40 Rxg7	Rc1+
41 Ka2	Rf1
42 Rxa7!	
Black resigns	

There is nothing to be done about
the devastating Ra8+. Notice how
the queen exchange robbed Black
of any chances.

The second principle is: *avoid
exchanges that lead to endgames
which are book losses*. I mean,
where is the percentage in heading
for an endgame which is a theoretical loss? An excellent first example
is from Diagram 139, A. Zapata–
J. Sunye, Cienfuegos 1984, after
Black's 41st move. The situation is
clear: Black momentarily is up two
pawns on the queenside, but White
can get one back by capturing the b-
pawn. How should he? 42 Rxb7!, of

course! Though Black retains a
clear advantage after 42 . . . Qe5+
43 Kh1 Rd8, the presence of the
heavy pieces gives White real
chances of survival. And, in any
case, he has no choice because after
the game's:

42 Qxb7??	Qxb7
43 Rxb7	Ra8!

. . . Black's rook is in the active
behind-the-passed-pawn   position
and the endgame is a clear theoretical win. The fact that White lasts
another twenty moves is immaterial, because his loss is certain.

44 Kg3	a5!
45 Rb3	a4
46 Ra3	Kg6
47 Kf4	Kf6
48 Ke4	Ke6
49 Kd4	Kd6
50 Kc3	Ke5!

A well-known strategy: while
White is busy on the queenside,
black's king will infiltrate the kingside. This same motif will also
appear in our next example.

51 Kb2	Ke4
52 Ka2	Ra6
53 Rg3	g5
54 Ka3	Ra8
55 Rf3	h5
56 Rg3	Ra5
57 Kb4	Ra6
58 Ka3	g4!
59 Rc3	Kf4
60 Rc5	gxh3
61 gxh3	h4
62 Rc3	Re6!
63 Kxa4	Re3
White resigns	

With White's king far away and
cut off, Black will capture White's
h-pawn and then easily queen his
pawn.

Even world class grandmasters
are not immune from such errors.
Witness what occurs from Diagram
140, V. Korchnoi–J. Timman,
Match Game 3, Hilversum 1982,
after White's 32nd move. The
passed b-pawn does give White a
clear and substantial edge. Yet
Black is not without prospects: the
b-pawn is at present securely blockaded and the fairly open position of
the white king gives Black chances
for counterplay with a potential
perpetual check in view if White

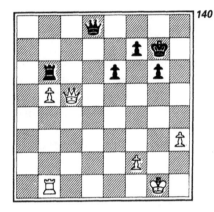

becomes too rambunctious. Therefore, Black should now play
32 . . . Qb8! with both defense and
counterplay in mind. Instead:

32 . . .	Qd6??
33 Qxd6	Rxd6
34 b6!	Rd8
35 b7	Rb8
36 Kg2	

While it is true that this endgame
is not as bad as that in the previous
example, it is bad enough to be lost.
Even though material is even,
about 99% of such endgames are
won for White because there is no
way to ultimately prevent White's
king from infiltrating. Again note
that White's rook—behind the
pawn—is active; Black's is most
passive.

36 . . .	Kf6
37 Kg3	Ke5

38	Kg4!	f6
39	h4	Kd6
40	Rb6+!	Ke5

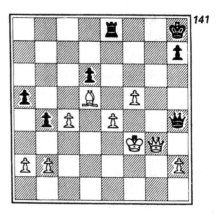

After 40 . . . Kc7 41 Rxe6 Black's kingside collapses and with his king cut off, so does the game; after 40 . . . Kd5 41 f4 the game continuation is reached.

41	f3!	Kd5
42	f4!	e5

Since Black's rook cannot move, nor the king (42 . . . Kd4 43 Rxe6 etc. again leaves the king cut off), a pawn move is required. Yet now White is able to fashion a second passed pawn.

43	f5!	gxf5+
44	Kxf5	Kd4
45	h5!	e4
46	Kf4!	Kd3
47	h6	e3
48	Rb3+	Kd2
49	Rxe3	Rxb7
50	Rh3	

Black resigns

In Diagram 141, N. Short–T. Horvath, Lvov 1984, after White's 44th move, White has a clear advantage since he has a powerful bishop and two good pawns for the rook. Yet after the logical 44 . . . Qf6! Black has chances for the draw because White's king is somewhat exposed.

Instead, unaccountably, Black played:

44 . . .	Qxg3+??
45 hxg3!	

While it is probably true that this position—or anything very similar—does not appear in any basic endgame text, still it is very easy to evaluate. White is sure to get two passed pawns and these in combination with the well-placed bishop and king must lead to a certain win. As it happens, White wins even faster because Black puts his rook on an awkward square.

45 . . .	Kg7
46 Kf4	Kf6
47 g4	h6
48 Be6!	Re7?!
49 c5!	Rxe6
50 fxe6	dxc5
51 e7!	Kxe7

52 Ke5
Black resigns

Our third principle is also very clear: *avoid exchanges if these are contrary to the theme of the position.* There is no better example than the one from Diagram 142, A. Ivanov–Y. Petkevichs, USSR 1982, after White's 13th move (after 1 e4 c5 2 Nf3 d6 3 d4 cxd4 4 Nxd4 Nf6 5 Nc3 e6 6 f4 Be7 7 Be3 0-0 8 Qf3 e5 9 Nf5 Bxf5 10 exf5 Qa5 11 0-0-0 e4 12 Qe2! Rc8 13 Qb5!). As can be seen

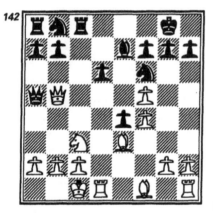

either from the moves so far—and from the diagram—we have a wild and wooly Sicilian with castling on opposite flanks and mutual attacks in the offing. It is imperative for Black to retain his attacking prospects and play 13 . . . Qc7!. Instead, after the non-thematic:

13 . . .   **Nc6??**
14 Qxa5   **Nxa5**

15 Bd4!

White wins the e-pawn for nothing and retains the better position. Black's prospects are nil and White wins by playing simple good moves.

15 . . .	Nc6
16 Bxf6	Bxf6
17 Nxe4	Bd4
18 g3	d5
19 Nd6	Rd8
20 Nb5!	Be3+
21 Kb1	Rac8
22 Bg2	Ne7
23 Rhe1	Bc5
24 Nxa7!	Ra8
25 Nb5	Nxf5
26 Nc7	Rab8
27 Nxd5	

Black resigns

Black also fails to grasp the correct theme from Diagram 143, M. Chandler–E. Kengis, Jurmala 1983, after White's 29th move.

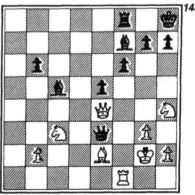

Black had earlier sacrificed a piece for two pawns and that is still the material situation, meaning that Black is a pawn down. He must look for compensation in the active location of his queen, acting in conjunction with the two bishops. The only move that makes sense now is 29 . . . Qd2!, thereby further activating the queen, pinning White's bishop and threatening to capture the b-pawn for material equality. Instead, Black played:

29 . . .	Qxe4+??
30 Nxe4	Bd5
31 Bf3	Bd4
32 Nc3	

In any kind of a normal endgame situation, two pawns are just not adequate for a piece. So here too, with White making good use of his extra piece.

32 . . .	Bc4
33 Rd1	f5
34 Bc6!	Bb3
35 Rd2	g6
36 Nf3	Rc8
37 Bd7	Rd8
38 Nxd4!	exd4
39 Rxd4	Be6
40 Rd6!	

Black resigns

After 40 . . . Bxd7 41 Nd5 f4 42 Kf2! fxg3+ 43 Kxg3! followed by 44 Nxb6 or 44 Nf6, the pinned bishop is lost.

The last important principle to always keep in mind is: *avoid exchanging if the queen is required as a source of potential counterplay.* There are just so many positions which are "dead" and *remain* "dead", unless potential life can be injected into them from the use of the queen. Such positions, if you exchange queens, invariably are lost. The first excellent example is from Diagram 144, L. Portisch–U. Andersson, London 1982, after White's 20th move. White here has

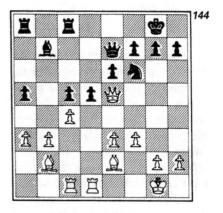

a substantial advantage: White's pieces are actively and harmoniously placed, he has the potential power of the bishop pair, Black's center is under unpleasant long term pressure and at this moment White—thanks to the Q + QB battery—is threatening 21 cxd5 (21 . . . Bxd5? 22 Rxd5!). Black must do something about the threat and the best defense is 20 . . . Qf8! which unpins both the e-pawn and the Knight. Of course, White's position remains superior, but Black can defend in the short term and with queens on the board there also always is hope for the future. Yet the correct 20 . . . Qf8! appeared too unsafe for Black and he chose a "safer" move, but one without any prospects for future salvation:

20 . . .	Qc7??
21 Qxc7!	Rxc7
22 Be5	Rcc8
23 cxd5!	Bxd5
24 Rc3	

The previous simplification has been all in White's favor: with the opening of the position the power of his bishops has been enhanced and both rooks are on key central files. Moreover, Black's isolated pawns on the queenside are vulnerable both in the long and short term and Black therefore now tries to exchange one of them. I evaluate that on an overall basis this position is already won for White.

24 . . .	Nd7
25 Bg3	a4
26 e4!	Bc6
27 b4!	cxb4
28 axb4	Nf6

Advancing the a-pawn just leads to a death sentence for it:

28 . . . a3? 29 Ra1 a2 30 Rc2.

29 b5	Bb7
30 Ra3!	Nh5
31 Bf2	Nf4
32 Bf1	

Black's progress has been cosmetic only and he will be chased back on all fronts. Also note that the further "active" 32 . . . Rc2? is refuted by 33 Rxa4!.

32 . . .	g5
33 g3	Ng6
34 Rd7!	Rcb8
35 Bd4!	g4
36 Ba1	h5
37 Be2	Ra5
38 Kf2!	Raa8
39 Ke3	gxf3
40 Bxf3	Nf8
41 Rc7	Bc8
42 e5	Ra5
43 Bc6	
Black resigns	

He is in a complete bind and White will start the decisive penetration with 44 Rd3.

A further example of the disease that I call "inviting in the undertaker"—and in a generally non-threatened position—occurs from Diagram 145, N. Short–C. van Wijgerden, Amsterdam 1982, after White's 27th move. White does have a clear advantage

145

because his pieces are much more active and, moreover, Black has a very vulnerable pawn on c6. Still, Black is holding on and after the simple retreat 27 . . . Kg8! he could hope, with careful defense, to survive. Yet again Black prefers "losing safely":

27 . . .	Qe5?
28 Qxe5+	Rxe5
29 Kf2	Rh8
30 Rd3!	

With the queens off, White's plan for winning is simplicity itself: he will play 31 Rc3 followed by 32 Na5 and capture the c-pawn. Black has no satisfactory defense.

30 . . .	Rd8
31 Nc5!	Re7
32 e5!	d5
33 Rc3	Nb6
34 Ra7	

The penetration by the rook ensures material gain.

34 . . .	Rb8
35 Rxb7	Rbxb7
36 Nxb7	Rxb7
37 Rxc6	Nc4
38 f4	Ra7
39 Rc5	Ra2
40 Bd3	Na3
41 f5!	Rb2
42 f6+	Kh6
43 e6!	

Black resigns

The f-pawn queens after 43 . . . fxe6 44 g5+ Kxg5 45 f7. Instructive how helpless Black's position became after the exchange of queens, yes?

There really should be no psychological problem in refraining from exchanging queens in positions such as Diagram 145. In dangerous looking positions the psychological factors are not so easy to brush off. Still, remember that chess points will go to the brave. If something inside is tugging at you to get you to exchange so as not to lose quickly, resist it, unless of course there is no choice. Just repeat to yourself "the worst that can happen is that I lose" —and keep the queens on! This little introduction brings me to Diagram 146, C. Hoi – V. Jansa, Esbjerg 1982, after White's 22nd move. White has the superior center, attacking chances against

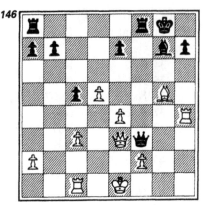

146

Black's king and prospects of winning Black's isolated e7 and h7 pawns. However, White's practical difficulties are considerable because his king is forced to remain in the center in a fairly open position. If Black now has the nerve to play 22 . . . Qg2!, White's task—both theoretically and practically—is most difficult, But after the "chickenish":

22 . . .	Qxe3+??
23 Bxe3	

White has a pleasantly won position. Black's weaknesses on e7 and h7 become vulnerable to exploitation and White's centralized king becomes wonderfully placed. The attempt by Black to defend his weaknesses by exchanging bishops just serves to turn White's king into a powerhouse.

23 . . .	c4
24 Ke2	Rf6
25 Bg5	Rf7
26 f4	Raf8

After 26 . . . h6 27 Bxh6 Bxh6 28 Rxh6 Rxf4 Hoi gives the following winning sequence: 29 Rg1+ Kf7 30 Rh7+! Kf6 31 Ke3! and Black's rook is trapped.

27 Ke3	Bf6
28 Bxf6	Rxf6
29 f5	h6
30 Rg1+	Kf7
31 Kd4!	

The active white king assures the win.

31 . . .	b5
32 Rhg4	Ke8
33 Rg7	Rh8
34 Kc5	a6
35 a4!	bxa4
36 Kxc4	h5
37 Rb1!	Kf8
38 Rg5!	Kf7
39 e5	
Black resigns	

As he was playing the forced 39 . . . Rfh6 Black overstepped the time limit. Of course, White then wins easily with 40 Rb7, threatening both 41 d6 and 41 f6.

26

Correctly Remaining in the Middlegame

Unless you are faced with some immediate calamity, you want to stay in the (unfortunately inferior) middlegame. The overriding reason for this is that it is not easy to play an errorless middlegame. Of course, this truth applies to you also, but what we are really concerned with is making things harder for your opponent. Yes, if you commit another error you will lose—but is it preferable to lose in the endgame? And if your opponent errs in a superior middlegame, your chances for a draw are great and if the error is serious enough, you even have a chance to win! Therefore, you are doing your best to make things difficult for your opponent—this is what successful practical play is about.

An enlightening first example is from diagram 147, G. Kuzmin – V. Cseshkovsky, USSR 1981 Championship, after White's 23rd move. White is up a pawn and threatens to get a decisive superiority with 24

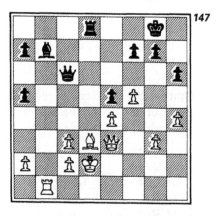

147

Qxa7. What should Black do? Obviously, he can take advantage of the pin on White's bishop to win back his pawn with 23 . . . Qxe4 24 Qxe4 Bxe4. Should he? Let us consider the endgame after 25 Re1. Black then has two reasonable choices:

(1) 25 . . . Bxd3 26 cxd3 f6 27 Rb1! with a large advantage for White because for practical purposes he is a passed c-pawn up, since Black's doubled a-pawns only have the value of one pawn.

(2) 25 . . . Bxf5 26 Rxe5 Be6 27 Rxa5 Rd7 28 Ke3 again with a large edge for White because he is ahead a pawn, the passed c-pawns are stronger than Black's extra kingside pawn and White has the more active rook + king.

Therefore the "tempting" 23 . . . Qxe4?! leads to nothing but a chanceless endgame. In the meanwhile White has a middlegame threat. Black finds the proper response:

23 . . .	Rd7!
24 Qxa7	

Otherwise it is difficult to see how White can progress, yet now the position sharpens considerably.

24 . . .	Qxe4
25 Qb8+	Kh7
26 Re1	Qg2+
27 Re2	Qxg3
28 Qxe5	Qxh4
29 f6+?	

And here comes the easy-to-make error. After the text Black gets passed g- and h-pawns which are secure enough, as is Black's king. Subsequent analysis showed that by 29 Kc1! White retains the advantage in a very sharp position.

29 . . .	g6
30 Rh2	Qg4

31 Qe3	h5
32 Kc1	Bf3!

Black is now both secure and better. However, both players have run short of time and this soon leaves its mark.

33 Rd2	Rb7
34 Ba6	Rb8
35 Rd3	Be2??

Black puts the bishop *en prise* to an unusual, though simple, discovered attack. After a normal sequence such as 35 . . . Bc6 36 Qe7 Qf4+ 37 Rd2 Bd5! 38 c4 Bxc4 39 Bxc4 Qxc4 40 Rd7 Qf4+ (Lukic) Black could have every expectation of winning. Instead, after the text move, it is he who loses.

36 Rd4!	Qf3
37 Qxe2	Qxc3
38 Rd7	Qxf6
39 Qe3	Rb4
40 Bd3	Rf4?!
41 Rd5	Rh4
42 Qe5!	
Black resigns	

In the endgame Black's pawns are too slow; in the middlegame he will get mated.

Equally instructive is Black's play from Diagram 148, M. Cebalo – P. Nikolic, 1982 Yugoslav Championship, after White's 26th move. White is significantly ahead in development, has a passed c-pawn and, moreover, Black's K + KR are at the moment awkwardly placed. Is not therefore Black's safest course to exchange queens? No, not as far as saving the game is concerned. Then Black would be without counterplay and not only would White's king be safe but it could even be of considerable help to the c-pawn. Black's coming play is a model of how to succeed by staying in the middlegame:

26 . . .	Qa5!
27 Rc1	Kh7
28 Qe4+	g6
29 h4?!	

Played without sufficient concentration. The attack on the kingside is not the key aspect in the position. Nikolic recommends immediate activation of the c-pawn with 29 c6! and after 29 . . . Rc8, 30 Re3.

29 . . .	Rb8!

with the dual threats of 30 . . . Rxb2+! and 30 . . . Rb4.

30 Qf4	Rhf8
31 h5	g5
32 Qe4+	Kg8
33 Qe5	Rb5!
34 Rc2	Rc8
35 Rec1	Rc6!
36 Qc3	Qa4!

keeping the queen active. As we will see the necessary counterplay will be supplied by the queen.

37 Rd1!	Rb8
38 Rd4	Qb5
39 f4?!	

This bit of carelessness is enough to give up White's advantage. The careful 39 Rc4 or 39 Qc4 were in order.

39 . . .	Qf1+!
40 Rc1	

After 40 Ka2?? Ra6+ White *loses*.

40 . . .	Qxg2
41 Rcd1	Kh7!
42 Qd3+	

White has nothing better than to go for the draw since 42 Rd8? loses to 42 . . . Qe4+ 43 Kc1 Qxf4+.

42 . . .	Kg7
43 Qc3	Kh7
44 Qd3+	Kg7
45 Qc3	
Draw	

Even in harmless looking positions, you want to think twice before exchanging queens. An excellent illustration is Diagram 149, W.

Browne – T. Petrosian, Las Palmas Interzonal 1982, after White's 22nd move. White has a clear advantage for two reasons: Black's d-pawn is forever vulnerable to an attack by White's bishop and White has control of the open e-file. Black cannot neutralize the latter factor with 22 . . .Qxe3?!+ 23 Rxe3 Re8 because White does not play 24 Rxe8+?! Nxe8 25 Bxd5 because Black (similar to the game) can successfully blockade with 25 . . . Nd6!, but instead 24 Rc3!

with a wonderful and easy-to-play endgame. White's rook then cannot be prevented from getting to the 7th rank and this in conjunction with the superior minor piece will be a very significant advantage. Instead, Petrosian — who generally has a reputation for "safety" — plays the more ambitious:

22 . . .   Qb4!

Staying in the middlegame does not decrease the white advantages enumerated above, but does make it much more difficult for White to *capitalize on them*. Remember, in inferior positions you want to make things as difficult as possible for your opponent!

23 Qc3!   Qd6!

Again Black should not exchange since after 23 . . . Qxc3?! 24 bxc3 all of Black's problems remain. Moreover, he cannot then play 24 . . . Re8? since after 25 Rxe8+ Nxe8 26 Bxd5 the change in White's central/queenside pawn formation gives him a won endgame.

24 Re5   h6
25 Kf2

White tries to progress in a "safe way" and this does not succeed. According to Petrosian, the correct plan is 25 g4! followed by 26 Kg2,

27 h4 and 28 g5. Yet note that this requires some exposure of the king and therefore Black would retain practical counterchances.

25 . . .	Rd8!
26 h4	Kf8!
27 a3	

Here 27 g4? is clearly wrong because of 27 . . . Nd7!.

| 27 . . . | Rd7 |
| 28 Qb4? | |

In going for the safe way, White commits an instructive error. Just because the exchange of queens was favorable for him earlier, he assumes that it is still favorable. Instead here White had to stay in the middlegame, with Petrosian recommending 28 g3! for a continuing advantage.

28 . . .	Qxb4
29 axb4	Ng8!
30 Rxd5	

After 30 Bxd5? Ne7 Black will have the advantage.

30 . . .	Rxd5
31 Bxd5	Ne7!
32 Be4	

Or 32 Bb7 Nf5! followed by 33 . . . Nd6. In either case, Black cannot be prevented from setting

up an impregnable blockade thanks to having a knight. Remember that the knight is the *premier blockader*! Petrosian has no further problems in holding the game.

32 . . .	Nc8!
33 Ke3	g5!
34 hxg5	hxg5
35 f4	gxf4+
36 Kxf4	f6!
37 Bd3	Nd6
38 Kg4	Kg7
39 g3	Kf7
40 Kh5	Kg7
41 g4	
Draw	

I shall conclude by showing how—by correctly staying in the middlegame—you can significantly increase your winning chances. Diagram 150 is A. Belyavsky – B.

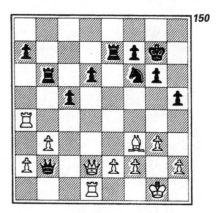

Spassky, Baden 1980, after White's 27th move. It is not an easy position to evaluate, yet I think that it is fairly clear that White's position is the more comfortable one. He has no structural weaknesses at all and his pieces are well placed. On the other hand, Black has an isolated a-pawn and a backward d-pawn. If Black now would play 27 . . . Qxd2? White could go about—uninterrupted—working to exploit Black's weaknesses. Spassky will have none of that:

27 . . .	Qe5!
28 h4	Rd7
29 Rc1	

White should strive to prevent the advance of the d-pawn. The best way is the immediate 29 Rc4!.

29 . . .	Rc7!
30 Kg2?!	

Now White is worse. Approximate equality is retained by 30 Qc3!.

30 . . .	d5!
31 Ra5	Qd6
32 Qb2	d4!
33 Rc4	Nd7!
34 Qc1	a6!
35 Rc2	Rb5!
36 Ra4	Ne5
37 Qf4	Re7
38 Be4	Re6
39 Bd3?	

Black's advantage derives from having greater central influence and some attacking chances against White's kingside. After the text move White already is lost. Correct is 39 f3 Rf6 40 Qg5 with White only slightly worse.

39 . . .	Rf6
40 Qe4	Ng4!
41 f3	Ne3+
42 Kf2	Nxc2
43 Bxc2	Qd7
44 Bd3	Qh3!
45 f4	

Black's attack is also decisive after 45 Bxb5 axb5 46 Ra7 Re6 47 Qc2 Re3! followed by 48 . . . Qh2+. In the coming play Spassky correctly goes for the middlegame kill, rather than settling for endgame superiority.

45 . . .	Rbb6
46 Bc4	Qh2+
47 Qg2	Rxf4+!!
48 gxf4	Qxf4+
49 Kg1	Rf6
50 Rxa6	Qe3+
51 Kh2	Rf4!
52 Qg3	Qe4
53 Ra7	Rxh4+
54 Qxh4	Qxh4+
55 Kg1	Qe1+
56 Kg2	h4
57 Rxf7+	Kh6
58 Rf3	g5
59 Bd3	Kg7
60 Bc4	g4
White resigns	

27

Exchanging Queens to Brake Your Opponent's Attack

Self-preservation is a necessity both in life and in chess. You must be able to withstand your opponent's attack so that "you can live to fight another day". The single most important strategy to blunt the attack is to exchange off the attacker's most powerful piece—the queen. Whenever you are under attack or feel that an attack is imminent, check whether the exchange of queens is in your interest.

This chapter will detail the circumstances when exchanging is the right strategy. First I will give two examples where the defender loses quickly because he avoids going for the endgame. Diagram 151 shows the position from M. Matulovic – G. Tringov, Titograd 1982, after White's 38th move. Black is a pawn down, yet since all the pawns are on the queenside and Black's two remaining pawns are sound, Black does not have to fear an endgame. The major problem that the missing pawn causes is a weakened king

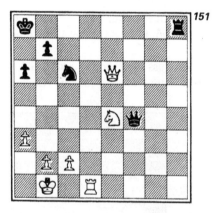

151

position. Based on the above logical evaluation, Black's correct next move is easy to find: 38 . . . Qe5!. If White exchanges, the endgame is theoretically drawn; if White moves his queen, Black has significantly improved the location of his queen *vis-à-vis* White's. Everything to gain, nothing to lose, is the message behind playing 38 . . . Qe5!. Yet Black did not play thus; instead he decided on a ridiculous attempt to attack White:

38 . . .	Qf3?
39 Rd3!	Rh1+?
40 Ka2	Qf1?
41 Nd6!	Na5??

The last chance was 41 . . . Qb1+ 42 Kb3 Na5+ 43 Kc3 Qe1+!, though Black has lost lots of time for the coming endgame.

42 Qc8+
Black resigns

It's over after 42 . . . Ka7 43 Qc5+ b6 44 Nc8+ Kb8 45 Qxb6+ etc.

No less instructive is Black's error from Diagram 152, A. Karpov

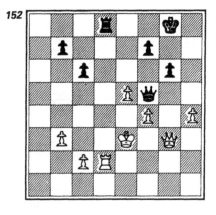

152

– K. Lerner, 1983 USSR Championship, after White's 41st move. White is a good e-pawn up and has attacking chances against Black's king. However, Black can enter a perfectly defensible endgame with the simple 41 . . . Rxd2!, e.g. 42

Kxd2 Qe4! 43 Qe3 Qh1! 44 Qf2. Because Black's queen towers over White's in activity, Karpov considers this Q and P endgame only slightly superior for White. Instead, Black played:

| 41 . . . | Re8?? |

Played according to the rule of thumb that "if down material, play for complications". Yet, this is specifically quite wrong here, because the complications are all in White's favor.

42 Rg2!

Lining up on the g-file *and* threatening a winning queen exchange with 43 Qg4!. The resulting R and P endgame is won for White because he has a good extra pawn and Black has no compensation or counterplay. Already Black is lost.

42 . . .	Qd7
43 h5!	Rd8
44 hxg6	Qd4+
45 Kf3	Qd1+
46 Re2	Qf1+
47 Ke3	f5
48 Re1!	Qb5
49 Qh3	Qc5+
50 Kf3	
Black resigns	

If 50 . . . Qc3+, 51 Re3.
Now we shall see the correct

application of the principle of self-preservation. If no defense to a coming attack is to be seen, do not commit suicide but head for the endgame. Even if it is very unappetizing, you are still alive and have something to hope for. Part of the time the hope is realized. An excellent demonstration of this occurs from Diagram 153, S. Gligoric – L.

153

Ljubojevic, Bugojno 1982, after Black's 19th move. Early on White had employed a very creative pawn sacrifice. Now with his next move White shows the point of this sacrifice.

20 Ne4!!

Black's queen is under attack and the only two reasonable plans are 20 . . . Qxc4 and the queen exchange. You surely want to look at 20 . . . Qxc4 first since it wins

another pawn and makes White's d-pawn vulnerable. White then plays 21 Nxf6+ gxf6 22 Rg1+ Kh8 23 Bb2!. Black must protect f6 and the two best ways of doing it are 23 . . . Rd6 and 23 . . . Qf4. Let us look at each of these: (a) 23 . . . Rd6 24 Qe2! and there is no reasonable defense against the dual threats of 25 Qe8+ and 25 Qe7; (b) 23 . . . Qf4 24 Qe2! and again Black is defenseless, e.g. 24 . . . Qd6 25 Qg2! or 24 . . . Bh3 25 Rg3!.

Therefore, since 20 . . . Qxc4? loses by force, Black's only rational choice is to exchange queens.

20 . . .	Qxd1
21 Nxf6+	gxf6
22 Rxd1	h5
23 Bb2	

White has a large advantage because of the passed protected d-pawn and Black's open king position. However, Black with perfect defense is just able to hold on.

23 . . .	Rd6
24 Rg1+	Kf8!

After 24 . . . Kh7? White penetrates along the e-file with 25 Rae1!.

25 Rae1	Bf5
26 Bc1	Bg6
27 Bh6+	Kg8
28 Re7	Ra6!

29 Bf4	Kf8
30 d6	Rd8
31 Bh6+	Kg8
32 Rxg6+!	fxg6
33 d7	Rxa4!

Even though things again look bleak for Black, it turns out that for the lost piece he gets two pawns. Moreover, with White's remaining pawns split, Black gets just sufficient counterplay to draw.

34 Re8+	Kf7
35 Rxd8	Ke7
36 Rc8	Kxd7
37 Rxc5	b6
38 Rd5+	Ke6
39 Rd4	g5!
40 Bf8	b5!
41 Re4+	Kf7
42 Bc5	bxc4
43 Kg2	

Nor is 43 Re7+ Kg6 44 Rxa7 Rxa7 45 Bxa7 c3 sufficient to win.

43 . . .	a5
44 h4	Ra2+
45 Kg3	c3
46 hxg5	fxg5
47 Rc4	c2
48 Rc3	
Draw	

A less extreme—but no less instructive—case of self-preservation is shown from Diagram 154, S. Dolmatov – V. Tuk-

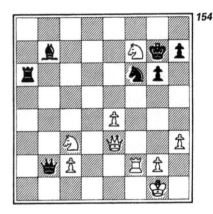

154

makov, Erevan 1982, after White's 28th move. White is already up two pawns and suicidal for Black is , 28 . . . Kxf7? because of 29 e5. What to do? Well, it is necessary to survive, so Black plays:

| 28 . . . | Qb6!! |
| 29 Qxb6 | |

The endgame will be defensible for Black, but under the changed circumstances, so is the middlegame after 29 Qf4 (29 Qh6+?? Kxf7 30 e5 Ra1+) 29 . . . Qd4!.

| 29 . . . | Rxb6 |
| 30 Ne5 | Re6 |

Black immediately wins back one pawn.

31 Nf3	Nxe4
32 Re2	Nc5
33 Rxe6	Nxe6
34 Kf2?	

Flustered by the unexpected dashing of his hopes, White gives back the second pawn. Correct is 34 Ne2!, when Black's chances for a draw are very bright, since White's c-pawn is difficult to mobilize and each side has only two pawns remaining on the kingside.

34 . . .   Bxf3
Draw

With 35 . . . Nd4 Black will capture the c-pawn.

If your opponent has sacrificed material to obtain a strong attack, aiming to exchange queens is logical for you in two ways. Obviously, it decreases the vehemance of his attack and, moreover, your chances of blunting it by giving back the material increases. This is well shown from Diagram 155, T. Petro-

155

sian – L. Karlsson, Las Palmas Interzonal 1982, after Black's 35th

move. For the sacrificed piece Black has two excellent passed pawns, a strong attacking position over-all and a very menacing queen. White correctly aims first at the latter factor:

36 Qb1!   Qxb1
37 Rxb1   e4
38 Re1   e3
39 Nxe3!

The exchange of queens has liberated Black's central pawns and thus White gladly gives back the piece to eliminate them.

39 . . .   fxe3?!

Short of time and surprised by White's lack of greed in defending, Black acquiesces to a routine recapture and immediately is left with nothing. As Petrosian subsequently demonstrated, Black could have retained the advantage with the perceptive 39 . . . Rg3! 40 Nf5 Rxe1 41 Nxg3 fxg3+ 42 Kxg3 Ra1! followed by going for White's vulnerable a-pawn with 43 . . . Nb3.

40 Rexe3   Ref8
Draw

Of course, you do not have to wait until you are in serious trouble before you start considering a queen exchange. The perceptive eye will start looking for it as soon as any danger appears on the horizon. This is beautifully demonstrated from Diagram 156, L.

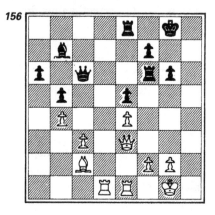
156

Psakhis – B. Abramovic. Tallin 1983, after White's 31st move. Because of the dark square weaknesses on black's kingside, White is threatening the very unpleasant 32 Qh6. Moreover, the attempt to prevent it by 31 ... Kg7?!, gives White the time for the strategically strong 32 Rd5!. Black finds the correct solution:

31 ...   Qb6!

Now White's queen is bound to defending the f-pawn.

32 Bb3   Bc8!

Preparing to neutralize White's bishop with a . . . Be6. Black is on the verge of equality.

| 33 Rd5!? | Qxe3 |
| 34 Rxe3 | Kf8! |

Instead, 34 . . . Be6?! allows 35 Rd6. Moreover, 34 . . . Rc6?! is inferior because of 35 c4! Be6 (35 . . . bxc4? 36 Ba4) 36 c5! and if Black accepts the exchange sacrifice, White gets two fantastic passed pawns and a clear advantage. After the carefully played text Black has equalized.

35 Rc5	Rd6
36 Rg3	Be6!
37 Bxe6	Rexe6
38 Rg5	Rd1+
39 Kh2	Rd3
40 Rg3	Rdd6
41 Rf3	
Draw	

If the pawn formation in front of your king is busted up, you are in continuous danger throughout the middlegame. The correct defensive technique is to decrease the risk to your king by exchanging queens. Watch how persistently this is pursued from Diagram 157, G. Kasparov – A. Belyavsky, 1983 Candidates Match, Game No. 1, after White's 31st move:

31 ...	Qe5!
32 Rg3+	Kh7
33 Qc4	

Black can protect himself after 33 Qg4 by 33 . . . f5 34 Qh5 Qf6.

157

33 . . .	Qe6!
34 Qd4	Qf5!
35 Qc4	

35 Rf3 is parried by 35 . . . Re4! 36 Rxf5 Rxd4 37 Rxf6 Kg7, with equality.

35 . . .	Qe6!
36 Qc7	Qe7!

Suicidal is the greedy 36 . . . Qxa2?? because after 37 b3! Black is defenseless.

37 Qc6	Qe6!
38 Qb7!	Qe7!
39 Qd5	Qe6!

Black is like a broken record. White therefore brings his queen to the kingside, but this allows Black to centrally activate his rook.

40 Qh5	Rd8!
41 Re3	Rd5!

Instead, 41 . . . Qd5?! allows White to remain in a pleasantly superior middlegame after 42 Qe2!

42 Qf3	Qf5!
43 Qxf5+	

White finally settles for a slightly superior endgame. There is nothing better since after 43 Qg3 Rd4! or 43 Qe2 Rd4! 44 g3 Qd5! Black's very active pieces give him full compensation for the kingside weakness.

43 . . .	Rxf5
44 Kg3	Kg6
45 Re7	Ra5
46 a3	Rb5
47 b4	a5
48 Re4	Rd5
49 f3	h5
50 Kf4	Rd3
51 a4	f5
52 Rc4	axb4!

Not 52 . . . f6? since after 53 b5! (Kasparov) White gets a favorable pawn formation.

53 Rxb4	f6!
54 Kg3	Rd6
55 Kf2	Re6!

Black's pawns are safe enough and his rook is active. White makes another try at winning by activating his rook, but Black parries it easily for the well-deserved draw.

56 g3	Kg7	61 f4	Rc5
57 Rc4	Kg6	62 Ra7+	Kg6
58 Rc8	Re5	63 a5	b4
59 Ra8	Kg7	64 a6	b3
60 Ra6	b5!	Draw	

28

Exchanging Queens to Minimize Other Troubles

As far as general principles go, the single most promising way to handle inferior middlegames is to stay in them while complicating matters as much as possible. Yet a one-track mind can never be successful in chess, because there is just too much variety and inexhaustibility in chess. In this, the last chapter, I will cover briefly other important situations when it is in the defender's interest to exchange queens.

If you can simplify into a theoretically drawn endgame, exchange queens. In other words, even if you have to give up material to escape from an inferior middlegame, if you reach the safe haven of a theoretically drawn endgame, do so! A perceptive execution of this principle occurs from Diagram 158, S. Cvetkovic – B. Parma, Sainte Maxime 1982, after White's 29th move. These kinds of positions are always clearly favorable for White because the major pieces provide strong attacking power and the extra pawn

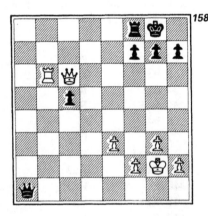

158

on the kingside both shelters White's king and can be used as a battering ram to help open up Black's position. On the other hand, Black's passed c-pawn has no real power since it is no threat to queen.

Knowing all of this, Black goes for an inferior endgame, but one which is known as a clear theoretical draw:

29 . . .   Qa8!

30 Qxa8	Rxa8
31 Rc6	h5!

The key to setting up a readily defensible R + 3P vs. R + 4P endgame is to prevent the stronger side from encroaching your position. Therefore it is very desirable to be able to advance your h-pawn two squares (to h5 if you are Black; to h4 if White is the defender). The position after the text move is a certain theoretical draw.

32 Rxc5	g6
33 h3	Kg7
34 f4	Ra2+
35 Kf3	Rh2
36 h4	f5
37 e4	fxe4+
38 Kxe4	Re2+
39 Kf3	Ra2
40 f5	Ra3+
41 Kf4	Ra4+
42 Ke5	gxf5
43 Kxf5	Rg4
Draw	

If it is the presence of the enemy queen that gives him the opportunity to exploit some strength in his position, exchange queens. This principle is well illustrated from Diagram 159, A. Belyavsky – Vl. Kovacevic, Bugojno 1984, after Black's 46th move. It is easy to see that Black is a passed a-pawn up and that both king positions are somewhat vulner-

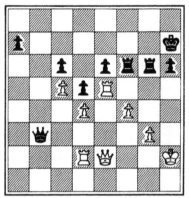

159

able. But the difficult part is: what should be White's plan/approach? "Conventional wisdom" would say that White wants to play for "complications" and that this surely requires for the queens to remain on. Yet a deeper look into the position tells us that it is the pressure against White's g-pawn and the generally active queen that gives Black excellent prospects of effectively mobilizing the a-pawn. Therefore White plays the unexpected:

47 Qd3!!   Qxd3

The resulting endgame offers Black no real winning chances. Yet also for the middlegame White has significantly improved his prospects.

48 Rxd3	Rg7
49 Ra3	Kg6
50 Ra6	Rc7
51 Kg2	

White's rooks are the active ones so that Black has no chance to do anything with his passed pawn.

51 . . .	Kf7
52 Kf3	Rg6
53 g4	Rf6
54 Re3!	Kg6
55 Kg3!	Kg7
56 Rea3	Rff7
57 Re3	Kf6
Draw	

If your opponent's edge in development is more menacing because he has a queen, exchange queens. Because the queen is such a powerful attacker it can add tremendous power to an existing edge in development. If your opponent's queen is more valuable as an attacker than yours is as a defender, exchange it off. Black is in trouble in Diagram 160, V. Hort – B. Toth, San Bernandino 1982, after White's

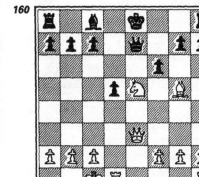

160

13th move (1 e4 e5 2 Nf3 Nf6 3 d4 Nxe4 4 Nxe5 d5 5 Bd3 Bd6 6 Nd2 Bxe5 7 dxe5 Nc5 8 Nf3! Nxd3+ 9 Qxd3 Nc6?! 10 Bg5! Nxe5 11 Qe3 f6 12 Nxe5 Qe7 13 0-0-0). White has a huge edge in development and Black has no fully satisfactory way of recapturing the piece. After 13 . . . fxg5?! 14 Qf3! Qf6 (Worse is the imitative 14 . . . Be6? 15 Rhe1 0-0-0 because of 16 Qe3! Rd6 17 Qxa7 Ra6 18 Nc6!! and White wins.) 15 Qa3! Black's king remains under severe pressure—analysis by Hort. Therefore Toth makes the correct decision: he will enter an endgame a pawn down, where the presence of opposite color bishops offers good drawing chances.

13 . . .	Qxe5!
14 Qxe5+	fxe5
15 Rxd5	Kf7!
16 Rxe5	Be6
17 Rhe1	Rhe8

As can be seen, Black has fully consolidated his position, though at the cost of a pawn. Yet under tournament conditions it is no easy matter for White to come up with the correct plan of what to do with his extra pawn.

18 f4?

Already White does wrong with it. This active, "logical" move makes it difficult for White to retain his kingside pawns "whole". Subsequently Hort suggested that the modest approach starting with 18 f3, to be followed by R1e3 and the king journey to f2, is the correct one.

18 . . .	g6
19 g4	h6!
20 f5	

Black also is safe after 20 Bh4 Bxg4 21 Re7+ Kf8! 22 Rxc7 Rxe1+ 23 Bxe1 Rd8! 24 Bb4+ Kg8 25 b3 Rd7!.

20 . . .	gxf5
21 gxf5	Bxf5!
22 Rxf5+	Kg6
23 Ref1	

Black gets sufficient counterplay after 23 Rxe8 Rxe8 24 Rc5 hxg5 25 Rxc7 Re2!.

| 23 . . . | hxg5 |
| 24 Rf6+ | |

The equalizer after the immediate 24 Rf7 is 24 . . . Re1+!

24 . . .	Kh5
25 Rf7	Rac8
26 Rg7	Re5!
27 b3	a5
28 Rff7	Rc5
29 Kb2	b6
30 a3	c6

Black's pawns are safe and so is he.

31 b4	axb4
32 axb4	Rc4
33 Kb3	Rf4
34 Re7	c5
35 bxc5	
Draw	

If your queen is awkwardly placed, exchange it off. If a particular problem for you is the lack of a comfortable location for your queen, then it clearly is in your interest to exchange it off—as long as you can do it at no cost. Looking at Diagram 161, P. Popovic – M. Cebalo, Vinkovci 1982, after Black's 20th move, we see that White's opening strategy is in shambles: White's central pawns have disappeared,

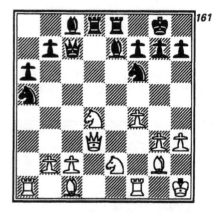

Black's rooks are on both open central files, Black has an over-all edge in development and White has kingside weaknesses. A further specific problem for White is the lack of a comfortable home for his

queen. Therefore, White quite correctly solves this problem:

21 Qc3!   **Qxc3**

The double attack on c7 and a5 gives Black no choice, since 21 . . . Nc4?? loses to 22 b3.

22 Nxc3   **Nc4**
23 Nb3

Of course, White is not rid of all of his problems, but at least he is rid of one. This gives him better chances for survival.

23 . . .   **Bf8**
24 g4   **b5**
25 g5   **Nh5**
26 Kh2   **Ne3**
27 Bxe3   **Rxe3**
28 Rf2   **h6!**
29 Nd5?!

Better chances of survival are offered by 29 gxh6 Nxf4! 30 Rxf4 Bd6 31 Nd5 g5 32 Nxe3 Bxf4+ 33 Kh1 (Cebalo).

29 . . .   **Rg3!**

With the threat 30 . . . Rxg2+!.

30 Nb6   **Bf5**
31 Rxa6   **hxg5**
32 fxg5   **Bd6**

White's position is most un-

pleasant. But think how much worse it would be if Black still had his queen!

33 Kh1   **Bxh3**
34 Nd5   **Bxg2+**
35 Rxg2   **Rh3+**
36 Kg1   **Bf8?**

Though White's position does remain most unpleasant, the absence of queens seems to allow him to hold off Black's attack. Therefore, Black should have gained material with 36 . . . Rxb3! 37 cxb3 Bc5+ 38 .Kf1 Rxd5 which in the long run must be decisive.

37 Nc3   **Nf4**
38 Rg4   **Rf3**
39 Ra1   **Rc8**
40 Nd4!   **Bc5**
41 Ncxb5   **Ne2+**
Draw

Exhausted by the tense struggle, the players called it quits in this unclear position.

If the enemy queen prevents you from exploiting your only hope, exchange it off. In an inferior position, you need some chance for counterplay. Otherwise, you will just be ground down. A quick look at Diagram 162, I. Farago – A. Sznapik, Belgrade 1984, after Black's 22nd move, is enough to see that the center and kingside is all Black's. White's only hope comes

162

from having a passed b-pawn but the chances of exploiting this are zilch as long as the queens are on the board. Therefore:

23 Qe6!!   Qxe6

Black has no good choice. Still, even after the exchange Black seems to stand famously. Yet White has understood the position very well.

24 Bxe6   Nxf4
25 Bc4!   Nd7

Perhaps giving the pawn back via 25 . . . d5!? 26 Bxf4 exf4 27 Bxd5 Nd7 offers better chances for a slight edge.

26 g3   Nb6

White can also defend after 26 . . . d5 27 Bb3! c4 28 Bxc4 dxc4 29 gxf4.

27 Be2!   Ne6
28 Ba5!!   c4

White also has sufficient counter-play after 28 . . . Rb8 29 Rf6; 28 . . . Nd7 29 b6; 28 . . . Rxf1+ 29 Bxf1 Nd7 30 b6.

29 Rxf8+   Nxf8
30 Bxb6   Bxb6
Draw

After 31 Bxc4 material is even and the presence of opposite color bishops will allow White to block-ade Black's central pawns.

Printed in the USA
CPSIA information can be obtained
at www.ICGtesting.com
JSHW021913100224
57071JS00001B/5